I0535849

Writers' Anthology Group

Serendipity

Copyright © 2013 the Authors and Bent Banana Books

Serendipity

All rights reserved. No part of this book may be reproduced, stored in a retrieval system, or transmitted, in any form or by any means without the prior written permission of the publisher, nor be otherwise circulated in any form of binding or cover other than that in which it is published and without a similar condition being imposed on the subsequent purchaser.

First published in 2013 by Bent Banana Books in association with the Writers' Anthology Group.

Visit *bentbananabooks.com.au*

Visit *www.artsalliance.org.au*

Bent Banana Books *email bentbananabooks@gmail.com*

24 Lorraine Court Lawnton, Australia, 4501.

Phone 617 3264 2311
Email peter@petercampbellrealty.com
Web www.petercampbellrealty.com

A CiP catalogue record for this book is available from the Australian National Library

ISBN 978-0-9805684-6-2

Cover graphic, Ken Armstrong

TABLE of CONTENTS:

TABLE of CONTENTS continued

Photographer: Marion MacLaughlin

FOREWORD BY BERNIE DOWLING

ON behalf of the Writers Anthology Group, based in the Pine Rivers district of Australia, I present our 2013 anthology, *Serendipity*.

This anthology follows three critically acclaimed volumes published by Bent Banana Books in conjunction with the Arts Alliance Pine Rivers. These anthologies were *The Writing on the Wall* (2010) *Can You Believe It* (2011) and *Sweet and Sour* (2012) Again we have short stories and poetry, illustrated by local artists, this year introducing photography.

Some writers and illustrators have been with us from volume one; others are newbies; we thank all for their contributions.

Authors range from people who earn or have earned a living from writing to those being published for the first time.

As with previous anthologies, the title is thematic of the contents. This year the challenge was to work with one word, not in common use: *serendipity*. You will read how that title has inspired a diversity of short stories and poetry.

In a country such as Australia, with a small population, government support of the Arts is crucial but such support ebbs and flows with changing political priorities and personal preferences of elected officials. As an alternative, a collective of writers and illustrators can produce quality books without undue financial burden on individuals. Any group from any country wanting some advice on replicating our initiative can email Bent Banana Books with details on the housekeeping page at the beginning of this book.

We acknowledge the work of our editorial panel: Bernie Dowling, Vera Murray, Anne Olsson, Lorraine Noscov, Ronald Holt and David MacLaughlin, as well as that of our cover designer/ illustrator Ken Armstrong.

We warmly thank our corporate sponsors Peter Campbell of Peter Campbell Realty, based at Albany Creek and Morayfield, and Bent Banana Books of Lawnton. Local business supporting grassroots arts and literature is inspirational.

Without further ado, let the literary gymnastics begin.

– Bernie Dowling, *WAG editorial committee*

SLAVES AND MASTERS
Margaret Taylor

THE woman was not listening to what her husband was saying, just noticing the redness of his neck and the way his head moved from side to side as he talked. He was not looking at her. His words were directed at her, not to her. She was sitting while he was standing, which made her feel at a disadvantage. He was telling her what to do. Again. Telling her not to interrupt, just listen, telling her she was not allowing him to speak, to explain, to have his say. Why did she feel it was always the other way around?

She felt trapped and tears began to form. She made an effort to hide them. Tears meant weakness and her husband would take advantage of that, becoming dismissive and scornful. He would know he had won again, making her feel even more inadequate, less in control of her life.

When he finished talking and walked away, she glanced at her coffee mug on the table. It was the mug that Maisie, her 11-year-old granddaughter, brought back from holiday a year ago, the one with a picture of Sydney Harbour Bridge on it. Staring at the mug she had a desperate urge to hurl it through the window. The thought gave her pleasure as she imagined it smashing through the window, making a crashing sound, leaving a gaping hole, shards of glass falling onto the floor. She enjoyed imagining the look on his face, in fact relished it, and held on to the thought for a moment. However, she knew it would never happen in reality because the consequences were too unbearable to think about. Besides, Maisie would be upset. The mug had been a present to her "special Nan". The woman folded her arms across her chest, rubbing the top of one arm in a consoling way.

It started early in the marriage and she did not tell anyone what was happening because of the shame. She wondered what she was doing to cause it. Reflecting on those earlier times she acknowledged, sadly, to herself that nothing had changed over the decades. Expressing an opinion or speaking her mind had never been an option. She learnt that doing so resulted in an angry outburst from her husband, leaving her confused and fearful. Keeping her thoughts and ideas to herself became a habit.

There were no broken bones or bruises but there were scars which no one could see. They were hers to feel. The scars were symptoms, the cause was words. Words were catapulted with accuracy to ensure maximum damage. Her gestures, facial expressions and mannerisms were mimicked and mocked. Words became the mechanism for control and power. How could words hurt so much? How could a look frighten her? How could she tell anyone what was happening when there was only words?

Lately she had become aware of her thoughts turning against her; criticising, deriding, blaming, belittling, chipping away at the core of her being, her spirit, and her soul. The thoughts were an echo of her husband's voice. Was there no escape from them? She wondered at times who she really was and searched for the intelligent happy woman she used to be.

Fear was a constant companion and had become her Master. Fear was always there, watching, waiting, ready to pounce unexpectedly. There were arguments without a reason, coming out of the blue, which left her feeling weak, bewildered and physically ill. She constantly had to think about saying or doing the right thing to avoid her husband becoming angry. At times she thought it was all in her imagination, or was all her fault and she must be doing something wrong. She decided to change her behaviour, to agree, to become invisible in order to make right whatever it was she was doing wrong. Only things were never right and she did not know why. She fought against the Master named Fear; fought not to let it take control of her but the struggle was constant, leaving her tired and puzzled most of the time.

One day she went into the shed where her husband was at his workbench.

'I've just made some coffee.' she said, holding it out to him. 'Thought you might like some.'

He did not look at her. 'Just leave it there,' he said, indicating the place with a small gesture of his head.

She put the coffee on the workbench within his arm's reach.

'NOT THERE,' he shouted. 'THERE,' banging his fist down in a space not so very far from where she had placed the mug of coffee. 'Are you stupid? Can't you get anything right?' He turned away from her, shaking his head.

Serendipity

The woman looked at the man and saw a stranger. She wondered how and why she had lived with this person for so long, always in fear, not feeling alive, cared for, or loved. Something stirred within her: an energy, powerful and overwhelming, which leapt like flames from place to place in her body. Her old Master, Fear, had been replaced by a new Master. This Master's name was Revenge. The introduction of this new Master caught her off guard, making her feel dizzy. To steady herself she put her hand on the workbench and it contacted a heavy metal object. She curled her fingers around it. Was this the answer to revenge?

Time shifted into slow motion, giving her unprecedented clarity. She looked around the shed and saw wood shavings in a corner where the man had brushed them; saw jars of nails, and shelves holding power tools; smelled the contents of the shed – oil, tools, rope, bike tyres, and car parts; saw cobwebs, no longer inhabited; looked at mowers, spades and rakes; noticed the paint tins, lids stuck with the congealed drips of their contents. She glanced at the untouched mug of coffee, rich, dark and exotic. She smelt its tantalising, beckoning aroma.

Silence was all there was now, save for the pounding of her heart. She tightened her grip on the heavy metal object. The new Master, Revenge, was urging her to action. The woman held her breath, watching dust particles floating in a beam of sunlight coming in through the small window. It seemed as if a long time had passed but it was only fleeting seconds. In those few seconds the woman became aware of an unexpected discovery. She thought it was something to do with the beams of sunlight but could not be sure. Whatever caused the discovery did not matter because it made her feel happy.

Her serendipitous discovery was the knowledge that she did not have to be a slave to the Master, Revenge. Indeed she did not have to be, nor want to be, a slave to any Master, of which there were many. She knew, without doubt, that she was her own Master. This new knowledge filled every bone, muscle, nerve, tissue and cell in her body with such exuberance that her perception of life and herself changed in an instant.

The man had yet to discover, as the woman had, that Masters such as Anger, Revenge, Jealousy, Hatred, Fear, and others abound, waiting to enslave and entrap a victim. The victim's armour against the Masters is that of choice; making the choice of becoming a Slave or becoming one's own Master.

_____ooo_____

THE woman released her grip on the heavy metal object and turned to walk out of the shed. She smiled to herself, a plan already formed. The plan needed her to take courage, but would reward her, in time, with the restoration of her eroded self-worth and identity. She would see the return of her strength, resilience and optimism. Her plan was to pack a small case and quietly leave her husband.

STORM
Anne Olsson

She tarried alone, a girl forlorn,
When rain began that desolate dawn,
Clouds amassed, the sky grew black,
As she watched alone from in the shack.

A wind untamed broke branches free,
As lightning struck a nearby tree,
The rusty roof bore torrents of rain.
The old cow path became a drain.

As wind cavorted without a care,
Rain-wet debris filled the air.
Rivers of mud coursed down the track
That ran beside the humble shack.

She heard a knock upon the door.
A man heaved in, begrimed and poor.
Gaunt and stooped was his aging form.
He begged for shelter from the storm.

She briefly nodded her proud head,
Then tensely faced the storm instead,
The wind grew wild; the rain increased.
The storm became a wrathful beast.

All that day the storm raged on.
They watched and heard its ancient song.
Then when at last it did abate,
The old man said, 'It's getting late.'

He swung his swag upon his back,
Then strode outside and up the track.
He called his thanks; she smiled and waved.
She now felt safe. The storm was braved.

DEEP RIVER

Ronald Holt

NEARLY 10 years had passed since that fateful night. Yet, even after all that time, no one had come any closer to solving the mystery of what really happened.

As an old detective of 30-years' experience in criminal investigation, I had been assigned by my Inspector to re-examine a number of cold case files and found this one quite intriguing. I had pondered over the confused set of facts for some time trying to make sense of them. Nothing really added up until I accidentally came across the missing piece in the puzzle.

One of the main problems for the original investigators had been that all of the witnesses offered differing versions of the events. All had been drinking heavily that night which had distorted their recollections. I tried to link the areas of agreement to see if anything stood out.

The only certainties were that John Lisicki, the town barber, had died under suspicious circumstances and the autopsy report could not positively identify the cause. The report recorded a high blood alcohol reading as well as other prescription medicines and unidentified substances in his system. While some combinations of alcohol and drugs can be lethal, this did not appear to be case. There must have been something else. Foul play was suspected. He was a single man in his 40s, lived a quiet life, kept much to himself and, apart from his work, did not have much other community involvement. He lived alone since the death, a couple of years before, of his elderly mother for whom he had been carer. Rumours about his sexual preferences were explored but nothing untoward emerged. On the surface, John Lisicki was a model citizen who was well respected by his clientele. He did not seem to have any enemies and there was no motive for his sudden demise.

Everyone had a theory, of course, ranging from alien intervention to conspiracy, but the truth had remained hidden. Many thought he may have overheard something at work and was killed because it was not for his ears.

The differing accounts extended to what John Lisicki said with his dying breath. Two out of the six witnesses said his last words were "deep river". This was eventually discarded as probably being drunken slurred speech due the lack of any such rivers nearby. If that was what he had actually said, no one could work out what it meant.

I flicked through his personal effects looking for any other clues when a slip of paper with his hand-writing on it fell out of an old diary. It appeared to read "Deep river" but on closer inspection, the break between the two words was after the second "e" rather than after the "p". The second word ended in an 'a' which, when looked at that way, read 'Dee privera'. The "p" looked like it could be a capital as in "P". What was that - a name, a brand, a place or something else? I was champing at the bit to follow this lead.

Criminal histories and driver's license checks proved fruitless so I turned to the local telephone directory. There it was, Dee Privera, a local resident living in a nearby suburb. Maybe I was on to something. I could not get there quick enough.

The neatly painted cottage was surrounded by a white picket fence and a colourful floral display. It looked like something out of a picture book. *Hardly the home of killer*, I thought as I opened the gate and walked to the front door. It displayed an old faded sign, *Dee Privera, Herbalist*.

My knock with the shiny brass knocker was answered by an elderly lady with snow-white hair, pulled back in a bun. She wore wire-framed glasses and was dressed in a crocheted shawl, a frilly white blouse and long dark skirt. I tried to find a word to describe my first impression but only "witch" came to mind. That was unfair and I chastised myself. A delightful old grandmother was probably more appropriate.

I introduced myself. 'Good morning. I am Detective Sergeant Colin Sloan from the Criminal Investigation Branch. I am looking for Dee Privera.'

'I am Dee Privera. I have been expecting you although it has taken you a long time to come,' she replied in a soft calm voice.

What did she mean expecting me, I thought. I did not know myself that I was coming until less than an hour ago.

'Please come in. Would you like a cup of tea?' she asked politely.

I followed her inside, glancing around the room which resembled an antique furniture shop.

I was not used to drinking tea with suspects although Dee Privera was not your usual murder suspect. I replied, 'No thanks.' She motioned towards an ornately carved dining table.

'Please sit down. You must be here about poor Mr Lisicki. So sad. He was such a nice man. Almost like a son to me.'

I was dumbfounded. I am not usually lost for words but Dee Privera was something else.

I nodded and allowed her to continue.

'Drank too much. I did warn him. It was his ego, of course. Mr Lisicki wanted to stay young so that someday he might find a lady to marry. He had to care for his elderly mother for many years and he never went out much except to work while she was alive. She was very demanding and he never had any real life of his own. His clientele were all men and he was too shy to ask any ladies out. Such a pity. He could have made someone a good husband.'

I observed three coloured bottles on the table and I wondered what they were. I finally found my voice. 'What do you think killed Mr Lisicki?'

'Well,' she said, reflecting upon what she was about to say. 'The newspaper said that he had been drinking before his death. I warn my clients not to drink alcohol with herbal medicines but I have never known anyone to actually suffer any ill effects if they do.'

'I presume Mr Lisicki was one of your clients,' I said, as she continued to ponder the cause of death.

'Yes,' she replied. 'He wanted something to help his shyness and to make him feel and look younger. He was vain about his looks. These are the potions I prescribed for him,' she said, pointing to the three coloured bottles.

I looked at the labels on the bottles. The white bottle read, *Fountain of Youth*. The red bottle's label read, *Passion*, while the third, a green bottle, said it was a hair elixir for external use.

'He had been taking the red and white bottles for some time without any adverse effects. He only started using the hair elixir shortly before his death. He wanted to sell the hair elixir in his barber shop. When I heard of his death, I initially blamed myself. But I knew my potions could not have caused his death and, as the newspapers suggested he was murdered, I felt, in some sense, relieved. I thought that the police may come to see me but no one came. I was not surprised when you arrived today even though his death was so long ago.'

'What ingredients do you use in your potions?' I inquired, trying to read the labels.

'Only natural herbs and vitamins. All government approved. My family were Gypsies and the formulas for my potions have been handed down from past generations. I have had considerable success and most of my clients come back.'

'Except John Lisicki,' I suggested.

'Yes,' she looked down as she spoke. Suddenly she looked up. 'Oh, my goodness, you don't think he could have drunk the hair elixir? It was for external use only.'

'My guess is that somehow the high level of alcohol he consumed, combined with prescription drugs and the herbal potions, and maybe the hair elixir, turned into a lethal cocktail. He was pretty drunk. He may have consumed the hair elixir in error.'

'What happens now, detective?' Dee asked fearing the worst.

'I will have to ask you to come to the station to make a statement sometime but in the meantime I will have these potions analysed in the lab.'

'I never meant to harm him. He was such a nice fellow.'

'I know. His death was probably an accident caused by what he chose to ingest. I do have to report to the coroner but at last we may be able to put his mysterious death to rest.'

As I walked back to my car holding the coloured bottles, I had a chuckle to myself. Not that John Lisicki's death was a laughing matter but at the thought of what the boys back at the station would think. Would I get a reputation of solving a cold case murder mystery where hair elixir was the probable cause? Deep river, Dee Privera, I mused – the missing piece in the puzzle.

SENIOR LADIES HEALTH WALK
Vera Murray

Oh dear! Oh dear!
It's barely dawn.
The sun's not up,
And I'm forlorn.

I hear a knock.
My friend has come
To walk ten blocks.
Where are my socks?

We're past our prime,
Know in our minds,
These walks a must,
To halt the rust.

In pre-dawn light,
We make a sight,
Thick pants, track tops,
Scarfs, gloves, long socks.

The air is crisp.
The breeze assists.
Our noses freeze,
We start to wheeze!

At first we jog,
So full of zest,
But gasp for breath
On each hill's crest.

We slow our pace.
We puff past stores,
As owners yawn
At their open doors.

In dawn's soft light;
From a new sun,
We push with might,
Now home's in sight.

Vera Murray

We say 'Hur-ray'.
She walks away.
I start to think
Of forty winks.

The joggers off,
The corns relieved,
I brush my locks.
I toss my socks.

From my bedroom,
I hear her roar.
'Morrow mornin',
We'll do more walkin'...'

I cannot hear the rest she says;
I'm 'neath the blankets on my bed,
But I mutter, 'I'll be ready.'
I'm not decrepit yet...NOT ME!

FROM FOREVER TO NEVER
Rebekah Dowling

TWO young men are carefully fixing up the red 1965 convertible Ford Mustang. Covered from head to foot in grease and sweat, they turn screws here and there with confident hands. Jeans that have seen better days hang from their hips. Rags, wire and other bits fill every pocket. Flies buzz around their heads landing every now and again on the left-overs of lunch: cheese and pickle sandwiches. The blue heeler sits lazily watching them from under the shade of a ghost gum as they tinker away in the stifling tin shed.

Voices rise and fall in a soothing hum, a cricket match playing over the old wireless. It's the Ashes and it looks like the Aussies have this year's games in the bag, again. They are both cricket fans and discuss the game in detail. Keith reckons he could have made the local team if he hadn't broken his arm in the Big Flood two years ago; his bowling hasn't been the same since. Joey hopes his game goes well on Sunday. Sharon is coming to watch, though he isn't sure she knows he's alive.

The conversation turns to the future, and they talk about staying in Barcaldine or moving away from all the small town crap. Joey's heard there's a fortune to be made in the Perth mines these days, but Keith likes the idea of droving up north, or, as his sister's mate's Uncle suggested, fruit picking along the Murray. They happily argue the merits and problems of each idea and finally decide that it's time for a swim. As they race each other to the waterhole in the back paddock, Keith knows they'll end up staying here forever.

BUT time is a slow river that erodes and drags away until people and plans change. Sharon whispers to Keith when they lie on the grass under the stars on warm summer nights. Joey makes his decisions and you make yours, just different decisions.

On the nights that Sharon is away, there comes a time when the wombats stop the grunts of mating and gum trees start whispering the old man river's secrets to the moon. On those nights Keith isn't so sure that it wasn't his fault. On those nights he looks up at the stars which reflect his childhood and wonders what Joey's up to. Then he goes into the house and puts on the telly, drowning out the world with the help of a VB beer or two, or three, especially if the cricket's on.

____ooo____

BURNT orange sky is slowly giving way to twilight as the dusty Ford makes its way home. Pausing every now and again to unlatch gates and check fences, Keith enjoys these quiet afternoons that bring a cool relief after the blistering heat of the wool shed. His very bones are tired and he doesn't have the energy for guilt. He can look around at his farm and be content.

Bob Dylan is singing about changin' times on one of Sharon's favourite records when he walks into the kitchen. He kisses her hello and gets himself a glass of cool water from the tap. He sits down at the small wooden table and she begins telling him about the kids' dramas from the day. He smiles at them but all he can hear is the song in the background offering only a wind-blown answer to change.

He looks out the window, up at the sky as though he believes that the answer might really be out there. But, if it ever was, it has blown away by now and he looks back to his wife. She looks at him sadly but she has given up trying to get a reaction out of him when he's like this and his melancholy threatens to overpower them both to create a bleak abyss where their souls used to be. The floor boards creak under her feet as she pulls herself away from the darkness. Joey is coming up to get the kids on Friday, she informs Keith heavily. He's taking them back to Brisbane for Christmas this year. Keith nods. She reminds him to say goodbye to them the night before if he's not going to be around when Joey arrives. He looks at her sadly. They both know he won't be. Joey and Keith have managed to avoid each other for the past seven years, each aware how fragile the wall of tolerance they'd built between them was. This year will be no different.

Sharon watches him walk out the back door and she wipes away silent tears. Keith loves her and is one of the best people she knows but sometimes she isn't sure that she made the right decision. Sometimes regret worms its way into her mind, whispering of her selfishness and threatening despair. Sometimes she's sure all he sees when he looks at her is the friend he lost.

Crickets chirp in the black night accompanied by the creak of the old rocking chair. Keith sits looking up at the stars. His eyes automatically settle on the Southern Cross before moving to Orion's Belt and Sirius. Joey's voice fills his head explaining that they had to remember which stars were which so they could always find their way back. They'd spent weeks studying books and camping out before realizing they only had to know the Southern Cross. The only problem after that was that they never got lost.

Until now, Keith can't help but add. Now the stars were no more than useless pretty lights. Joey had been lost to him, beyond starry aid, the day he walked out that door and Keith had decided not to follow. Better to forget the Joey who belonged in his past. A frog's croak leaps through the shadows of Keith's mind and he slowly walks back inside to his wife and his future.

_____ooo_____

JOEY speeds up the driveway, the dirt track covering his shiny Holden in layers of dust. He loves the adrenalin rush this country can still give him. As fresh air, with only specks of stray dust, rushes into his lungs through the wide open windows, he lets out a whoop of glee. He lets his mind go blank before the memories rush in to remind him that this is no longer his town. He's a city boy now – a city boy who loves his street lights, the casino, cushy office job and, best of all, neighbours who know nothing about him.

As he catches sight of the old Queenslander through the trees he remembers that he didn't want the country life. Sharon, the kids, the farm: that was the life his parents expected him to have, the life everyone in that damned place lived. So he had got out. And when he did there was good ol' Keith, the stable serious best-friend, ready to step up and take his place. Too ready.

As Joey walked up the drive he remembered the fury he had felt when he came back that first time and had seen Keith in his house, with his kids, his wife.

His psychiatrist said it had been shame that made him do it. But Joey knew it wasn't. Because the first thing he'd felt when he'd seen, through the window, Keith lean down to kiss Sharon's head was fear. Dark, embarrassing, mind-numbing fear. The only thought in his head as he dragged Keith outside the house and pounded him into the dirt was that they couldn't be together. Because, if Sharon and Keith had each other, they wouldn't need him. That had scared him more than anything in the world.

SHARON slowly turns around at the whine of the fly screen door. She steadies herself against the big wooden table. Joey had always been handsome enough to take her breath away. When they'd first started dating she'd been on a constant high from lack of oxygen. But these days it was more embarrassment that made her heart race. He had been her first love. She knew him like the back of her hand. His rejection was the most shameful thing that had ever happened to her.

She greets Joey in the distant calm voice she has purposely reserved for him. And he tells her about business things that she doesn't really understand or care about. The conversation drifts to the kids and, when she accidently mentions Keith, each pretend it isn't a big deal.

'How is he anyway?' Joey asks, aiming for a casual manner and just managing it. Sharon thinks of Keith's sadness the other day and the boisterous *500* card game the family all played last night. She isn't quite sure how to answer so goes for a non-committal smile and a joke about a mid-life crisis. Joey's sharp look reminds her that mid-life crises aren't much of a joke for them so she laughs awkwardly and calls for the kids. 'They're probably playing in the creek bed, shall we go fetch them.'

Joey follows her out the back door telling her a story about one of his own creek bed adventures, deftly avoiding Keith's name.

The kids' blissful innocence always makes conversation easier and the walk back to the house isn't nearly as awkward. They tell Joey about the foal down the road and the Farrington's new motorbike and beg him to come see the go-cart they built with Keith.

The shed is a shrine to ages gone past. Dust and spiders fill every corner and memorabilia lines the shelves, stuffed between tins of paint and boxes of screws. A warm breeze toys with a decaying photograph lying next to the battered wireless on the floor. Joey, picking up the photo, is confronted by his own tan face beaming up at him, above an arm thrown around a sunburned Keith. The kids pull on his arms to see it and he tells them the story of two best friends who were sure that the Nazis were going to invade. They had spent every waking moment preparing, losing themselves in hidden trip-ropes, camouflaged holes and stink bombs. However after a few weeks his mum fell into one of the larger cow poo booby-traps and that adventure had come to a sudden stop.

Joey smiles at his children as they split their sides with laughter. He feels a dull ache in his throat as he remembers those days when he and Keith had been kings and fire-fighters. But childhood ties had stopped mattering a long time ago, he tells himself. Adults don't play imaginary games and friends don't turn their backs on you.

On the road out of town a glossy Holden and a rusty Ford pass each other, drivers carefully staring straight ahead. The laugh of a kookaburra is carried past on the warm summer breeze. But the two sad middle-aged men don't hear it amongst the roar of their engines and the clamour of memories.

YUSEF BOY
Bernie Dowling

Oh, Yusef boy, the cops, the cops are calling
From Labs to Libs, and down the racist slide.
The summer's gone, and all the goodwill's a dying
'Tis you, 'tis you must go and I must hide.

But come ye back when summer's in Cronulla
And when the rabble's hushed and done with blows,
'Tis I'll be here in sunshine or in duller.
Oh, Yusef boy, oh, Yusef boy; I love you so.

And if you come, and all the deejays are braying,
If I am dead, as dead I well may be,
I pray you'll find the place where I am laying
And kneel and say an "Allah" there for me.

And I shall hear, though soft you tread above me
And all my grave will warm and sweeter be.
And then you'll kneel and whisper that you love me,
And I shall sleep in peace, asylum come to me.

Oh, Yusef boy, the cops, the cops are calling
From Labs to Libs, and down the racist slide.
The summer's gone, and all the goodwill's a dying
'Tis you, 'tis you must go and I must hide.

JASMINE COTTAGE

Anne Olsson

I STRODE up the road, the address written clearly on the slip of paper in my hand – *22 Lavender Lane*. Each of the locals I had approached for directions had eyed me suspiciously, and had been reluctant to help. I was determined to find it however, and I did. It lay on the outskirts of the town, at the end of a quiet lane, bordered on both sides by a forest of cypress trees. There were no other houses in the immediate vicinity.

The sign read *Jasmine Cottage*. An aura of the inscrutable hung over the old place, apparently abandoned and neglected for many months. The windows were clouded with dust. Several panes of glass were cracked. Cobwebs hung from the eaves. The garden was overgrown, rank with weeds and dying plants.

It was not what I had been expecting. A sigh of disappointment escaped me. My spirit quailed at the sight of the neglected state of the building. This was the house I had planned to make my home!

Serendipity

I did not know who my mysterious benefactor was. I had hoped to find some clue to this inside this cottage. My divorce had left me emotionally debilitated and without a home. I had to make a new life for myself. When I learnt that I had inherited a house in a small country town, it had seemed to be the answer to a prayer.

Now, as I stood with my hand on the gate, tears of tiredness wet my cheeks. I thrust the gate open and pressed my way through branches that overhung the path. I turned the key in the lock with difficulty. As I pushed the door open, a musty smell smote me. As I stepped into the hall, it was as though I had been transported into another world.

The house was dark and oppressive. Faded curtains were drawn across the windows. The ancient furniture was shrouded with thick layers of dust. Pictures from another age hung on the walls. A cockroach scurried away at the sound of my footsteps. I walked dejectedly from room to room. When I returned to the dining room, I dusted off a chair and sat down in a daze.

How long I sat there, I do not know. I stood up abruptly when I felt a tangible presence in the room. 'Is anyone there?' I called as I turned around.

There was no one to be seen. I was not anxious, but I realised that I was very tired and disorientated.

I opened the back door that led into the garden behind the house. Here I found the remnants of an old vegetable garden. An aged poinciana tree was heavy with blossom. A carpet of red flowers lay beneath its wide-spreading branches. It was beautiful. I felt my spirits revive.

When I re-entered the cottage, I went into every room and drew back the heavy curtains. Light flooded in and suddenly the house seemed a little more cheerful. 'Yes,' I thought, 'I have a lot of work in front of me, but I will not shirk it.'

In the days that followed, I opened up the cottage to allow fresh air in to chase the mustiness away. I dusted and scrubbed the house vigorously. I arranged for the broken window panes to be replaced. I removed cobwebs and washed the draperies and bed linen. I polished furniture and shampooed carpets. At the end of each day I collapsed onto a bed exhausted, and slept deeply. Slowly the house was coming to life.

I received no visitors during this time, and my friendly overtures to other townsfolk when out shopping were met with coldness. I was bewildered by this, but I was too busy to give it much thought. I was weeding the garden beds in the front yard one day, when a cheerful voice greeted me. I looked up eagerly to see a middle-aged man smiling down at me.

There was nothing handsome about his face. It was dominated by a large craggy nose. His untidy mass of hair was flecked with grey. His deep-set eyes were sharp and piercing. Yet his smile was warm and genuine.

'Hello', I responded. 'It is nice to see a friendly face.'

'I'm Wayne Unwin, the local vet,' he said. 'I gather the locals haven't extended the hand of friendship to you?'

I looked at him thoughtfully. 'Well, no, I haven't received a particularly warm welcome.'

'You mustn't mind the folk here. They know who you are. In a small town, news travels fast. They'll get to know and trust you in time.'

He reached across the gate and shook my hand. 'They've always viewed this house suspiciously,' he explained. 'Was **Mrs** Ainsworth a relative of yours?'

'Was she the lady that lived here? No, I didn't know her, nor why she left me her house. It's been a mystery to me.'

'The locals were always suspicious of her. They believe she was responsible for the death of a child. They think she haunts the cottage still.' He looked up at the house with interest. 'Dotty was ill for a long time before she died. She couldn't care for this place properly. But you've done wonders here in a short time.'

He passed me a business card. 'Here is my phone number. I've been called out to a farm nearby, so I must be on my way. But if you're free tomorrow afternoon, you might like to get together for a cup of tea, and I can tell you more about the place.'

I thanked him warmly. I was sorry to see his gaunt form walk away.

I met him at his surgery the next day. As we walked back to his house, I was conscious of curious glances from people passing us on the street.

'Yes,' he laughed, 'you're the object of their curiosity. They assume you're a relative of **Mrs** Ainsworth. Give them time to get to know you.'

I felt uncomfortable under their scrutiny but I wanted to hear more of my benefactor.

We sat opposite each other at his kitchen table. He had placed two mugs and a generous pot of tea before us.

'Mrs Ainsworth kept to herself. And she was an advocate for homoeopathy... heaven forbid! That was enough to create suspicion in the eyes of the community.' He smiled. 'Dorothy was her name, but I called her Dotty. She had no family that I know of. She brought her cat into my surgery occasionally, and we became friends. She was an interesting woman. She was unfairly blamed for the death of a young boy she'd been treating for scarlet fever. She was cleared of all wrongdoing but many continued to believe she was responsible and ostracised her.' He grinned. 'Now they are convinced she haunts the cottage.'

Wayne began to visit me at the cottage occasionally when out on his rounds. I enjoyed his company. I was grateful for his kindness towards me, but he could not solve the mystery as to why **Mrs** Ainsworth had left me her home. Why me? Why she had chosen me of all people? What threads bound our lives together?

Wayne was intrigued about this too. He questioned me about my family.

'My parents **are dead**,' I told him. 'I've an older half-brother who lives in Perth. I phoned him when I first learned of the inheritance, but he was as mystified about it as I was.'

'What of the legal firm who handled Dotty's will?'

'They were under instructions not to disclose any information about her. I didn't even know her name.'

'Well, it is all very strange,' he commented. 'I never considered Dotty a secretive person. She always seemed so calm and sensible.'

My house was now clean and light and welcoming. The garden had been tidied and new plants were thriving under my care. I was growing vegetables in the old beds in the back yard. I was enjoying my deepening friendship with Wayne and my life had taken on a new meaning. Some of the locals would now acknowledge me in the street. I was beginning to appreciate my life at Jasmine Cottage.

One wet and grey Sunday afternoon I walked into one of the bedrooms when one of the pictures unexpectedly fell off the wall. I was mystified. It had been securely hung. I had dusted this picture before but never looked at it closely. I picked it up now and looked at it intently.

In the gentle face of the young woman in the photograph I saw intelligence and dignity. I turned it over. The words 'Dorothy Ainsworth' were inscribed on the back. So this was Dotty. As I stood gazing at the photograph, I felt a sudden chill in the air. I looked up. I sensed a presence in the room, the same strange sensation I had experienced on the day I had arrived at the cottage. I did not have a morbid imagination but I was disconcerted.

Uneasily I hung the picture back on the wall. As I turned away, I saw the old roll-top desk sitting in a corner of the room. I had only the day before discovered the key to open the desk. Though I had dusted and tidied its exterior, I had had no opportunity to study its contents. I felt an urge to do so now. A wet day like today would surely be an ideal time to do it?

I walked into the kitchen, prepared a hot cup of coffee and carried it back to the bedroom. Seating myself at the desk, I rolled back the lid and began to explore its contents. There were old bills, bank statements, account books and records of land valuation. I found an old exercise book containing scraps of poetry. Had Dotty written these?

Beneath a bundle of old letters there was a large envelope inscribed with one word – 'Will'. Was this Dotty's will? I opened the envelope hesitantly. As I unfolded the sheets of paper it contained, my hands shook. I read, 'The last will and testament of Dorothy Grace Ainsworth....' Was I to find out the truth at last?

I skimmed through the instructions regarding the payment of her debts and funeral expenses and the details of her executor. 'I leave my entire residuary estate to my grand-daughter Eileen Jane Roberts...' Her grand-daughter? No, there must be some mistake. I was not her grand-daughter. I remembered my grand-parents well. I had loved them dearly. I was confused.

The rest of the will gave me no more revealing information. I folded it and placed it back in the envelope. I felt too restless to stay in the house. I picked up one of Dotty's old umbrellas and walked out into the rain. I walked until the growing darkness forced me to return.

I was still confused. I did not sleep well that night and rose from my bed unrefreshed. There had to be some explanation for this.

The rain continued into the next day. After a meagre breakfast, I went back to the desk and studied the will again. What did this mean? Her grand-daughter? I searched through the bundles of papers on the shelves more thoroughly but found nothing to enlighten me. I came upon an old diary in a bottom drawer. Within its pages I found a letter. It was addressed "To my grand-daughter, Eileen Roberts". The eyes in the photograph on the wall seemed to be watching as I carefully slit the envelope open.

'Dear Eileen', she wrote, 'By the time you read this I will no longer be resident on this planet. I hope the contents of this letter will not grieve you. I am very sorry that I never had the opportunity to meet you but I hope you will learn to love Jasmine Cottage as I loved it and make it your home.

'How is it that I claim the right to call you my grand-daughter? I want to explain this to you now, and I hope you will not judge me. Your mother Elizabeth was my child, born out of wedlock when I was young and in love with the man who was your natural grand-father. When I told him of the pregnancy, he refused to take any responsibility for the child when it was born. He left the district shortly afterwards.

'When my parents discovered my predicament, they forced me to give up my baby for adoption immediately after the birth. At that time it was a great shame for an unmarried woman to give birth to a child. I was grief-stricken, both by the betrayal of the man I loved and the loss of my baby. In the years ahead I never married, but, after a long search, I discovered who had adopted Elizabeth. I moved to the neighbourhood where she was growing up, and watched her from afar. She only knew me as a distant family friend. I never revealed myself to her, and I don't think she ever knew that she was adopted.

'She married a good man who already had a son. They were very happy together. I decided it was time to let her go and moved away from the area. I had lived through and for her, too long. When I moved into Jasmine Cottage, I began a new life here. When I heard

31

she had had a child, a little girl, I was gratified that she knew the joy of raising her daughter, the joy I had never known. I was very sad when I found out that she had died, but I knew she lived on in you.

'I hope this does not come as a shock to you. Though you have never met me, yet I claim you as my own. I want you to know me as your grand-mother for I love you and have cherished the thought that perhaps you too will find happiness in this home in which I lived.

'My beloved grand-daughter, I know I go soon to a world beyond this world. Please do not judge me. If you can learn to cherish my memory after I am gone, as I have cherished you, you will give me all that I could ask for.

'With deep love,

Your grand-mother,

Dorothy Grace Ainsworth.'

When I lay the letter down upon the desk, tears welled in my eyes. I took the photograph of Dotty down. 'No, Dotty,' I said as I looked into her eyes, 'I do not judge you.'

I gently kissed the face of the woman in the photograph, and hung it back up on the wall. As I did so, the heavy curtains inexplicably billowed out into the room. The bedroom door slammed shut **unexpected**ly. A cold tremor tingled up my spine. There was again a palpable sense of a presence in the room. I smiled. 'It's only Dotty,' I whispered.

GRANDAD'S TEETH
Vera Murray

Granddad hunched and clutched his knees,
As the mighty sneeze exploded.
His teeth flew out his open mouth,
As if his grey haired head was loaded.

It spread his germs throughout the house,
To each ceiling, through each door.
All the family tried to shelter, or to hide,
From this flu they can't ignore.

Through his double yellow gums,
Granddad swore, Granddad spluttered,
'Where's me teeth? Where have they gone?'
'The grandkid took 'em,' he then uttered.

Granddad didn't have a clue,
That the family dog had carried 'em,
Down behind the outside loo,
And there it was he buried 'em.

'Go, get a new set,' we all said,
But he's too tight-fisted, you see.
So now we feed him soup and sops,
While we all feast on fruit and chops.

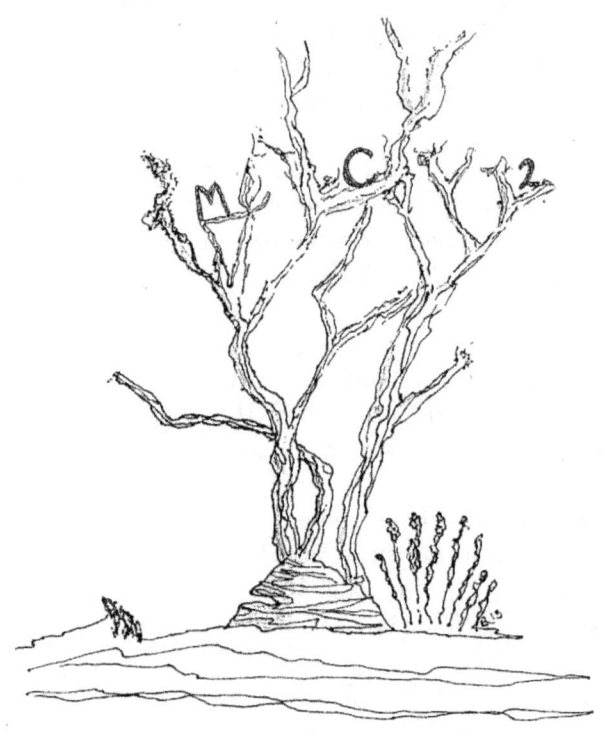

The Tree of Knowledge

BUSH HERITAGE AMBUSHES
THE CITY SLICKER
David MacLaughlin

Brisbane Australia, April 2013

THE chase was on. John was frightened out of his wits. The whole thing was more like a Dan Brown novel than a normal investigative journalist's assignment.

He dragged his long body into the small plane and stroked back his fortyish greying hair while slumping into the seat with a window view. His mind was racing as he collected his thoughts on his current reporting project. The country was in turmoil politically as Government, the trade union movement and mining leaders were at logger heads over a carbon tax, industrial relations and even Indigenous land rights. A deadly shroud of secrecy from all parties had enveloped the country into a battle of minds over the future direction of Australia. Even worse, people were mysteriously missing, presumed dead. John's investigative search had led him to seeking some connection to the Tree of Knowledge in Barcaldine. This tree represented the birth of the Labor Party in Australia.

John knew he was being followed so he was trying to give any pursuers the slip.

He had been given the tip-off to visit historic Barcaldine a few days earlier when he was in the Queen Street Mall. He noticed that someone was waving to him from one of those small charity stalls that had a spot opposite the casino. He went over to the stall which turned out to be an environmental tree-hugger group. She was in her thirties and attractive in a country-style way with loose fitting clothes and tousled blonde hair. She leaned towards John and whispered earnestly, 'Go to the Tree of Knowledge in Barcaldine and you will find why our country is in turmoil politically.'

What better way than to take a small plane over 1000 kilometres to a small town in western Queensland to achieve two goals. One was to get rid of anyone who was following him and the other was to, maybe, locate any secret material that the miners and Government were hiding. The Tree of Knowledge was the perfect place to hide files. Sounded farfetched, he mused to himself, but

Barcaldine had a violent past. Who knows what resentment still smoulders in the town over past injustices?

After two hours flying over vast mining areas and cattle country, the plane landed on the outskirts of the town. He had booked himself in at one of the many old wooden hotels that had survived to this day. His choice was the *Shakespeare*, not that he liked the Bard all that much but more that the old notion of British imperialism lived on in the bush in the form of a country pub. If anyone was following him he had to make sure he got rid of them so he could snoop around the Tree of Knowledge and find some link that the government, unions and miners did not want the country to know about.

He slept lightly as the pub's wooden floor boards and walls creaked and groaned while the night wind whistled through the building. Up early the following day and, after a "light" country breakfast of bacon, steak and eggs; he headed for his Cobb and Co coach ride into the bush. Could his dreaded follower be among his fellow coach riders? It did not seem so. They were a mixture of families with children; Grey Nomads swapping the caravan for a wild ride on an old coach and a few overseas tourists with Nikon cameras and souvenir T-shirts. What a ride it was, four horses galloping through the bush and dragging a large wooden coach with people inside and on top all hanging on and breathing in the fresh country dust rising from the thundering hooves of the well-fed horses. *That hairy ride would deter anyone who might be following me*, John mused to himself. He got off the coach and devoured morning smoko of damper and hot tea.

Making his way to the wooden railway station which was alongside the Tree of Knowledge, he passed elderly ladies playing croquet on the town-common pathway. They invited him to join them in a game. The more he behaved as a local the more he would not be followed; anyway that's what John thought as he belted his way around the croquet hoops.

The ladies conversation surprised John. 'Have a look at the Tree of Knowledge tonight with all the lights on the tree and in the crypt section,' one said.

'It's full of secret signs, they reckon and spooky too,' added another.

'It's all genuine, just like the Loch Ness monster, dinky di, it is,' a third said.

Were they prophesying like the witches of Macbeth? Who knows, thought John, as he re-traced his steps to the Tree of Knowledge.

The tree looked disastrous in daylight. The remains of the tree, poisoned by unknown people with glyphosate in 2006, had its dead branches stark and fossilised. The tree roots were encased below the level of the footpath in a see-through glass tiling in a manner of the Louvre in Paris. Who would have thought Paris and Barcaldine had anything in common? Then again, Barcaldine had Shakespeare. Fact is stranger than fiction. The best entry he could see to the crypt was by manhole and ladder. He would have to enter very late at night when nobody was around. In Barcaldine, this was usually the case after 6pm but you just never knew. He would need to be careful.

After a hearty steak dinner among the boisterous bunch at the pub, John waited in his hotel room until late and then ventured out. It was quiet. The Tree of Knowledge, sheathed in its huge modern black wooden hood, looked startling in the moonlight. The stars were clear and the Southern Cross seemed to be directly overhead the Tree's ornamental hood. He walked up to the tree marvelling in the interaction of the coloured lighting effects that had been wound around the dead tree. A new replacement tree had been picked but it was not large enough to be placed in the poisoned tree's place. The starry Southern Cross pointed through the top of the surrounding trees and connected up with a section of the tree roots visible in the underground crypt.

John's heart and brain were racing. Could it be that documents were hidden near the roots or in the marble beneath the footpath level? Everywhere was dead quiet. He must get into the crypt and examine what was there. Slowly he lifted up the entrance gate and began to descend into the cavern.

He stopped. Hearing nothing, he continued and let the metal grate close behind him. The cavern-like area was well lit in the centre but he headed for the far edge which was in shadow. He heard the sound, like a clap of thunder, of the grate opening and being slammed down again. The metal ladder rattled with the hurried feet of someone on it. *Hell*, thought John, *what's going to happen now*, as he vainly sought refuge where there was none. *I am trapped here with whoever has been following me.* A large shadow loomed and the sound of heavy boots on metal swamped his brain as a flashlight blinded his eyes and he heard a rasping voice exclaim, 'What the hell are you doing here?'

John squinted and avoided the strong torch light to see his follower was wearing blue clothes. His nimble brain thought of one thing: Police. *What the hell are they doing following me?*

The torch switched off as the voice in blue spoke rapidly. 'I am from the Queensland Police Intelligence Unit and you have been leading us a merry dance. The Feds want to lock you up as they think you're a danger to national security.

'We know you're too thick in the head for that but by accident your reporting assignment has stumbled on some politically sensitive areas. You're in danger so watch your step in future. We can't keep playing nursemaid for ever, you know.'

John stood up, heaved a sigh of relief and thanked the police agent for his info.

The police officer spoke less sternly. 'Great, I will keep in touch with you but I have a feeling that in Barcy lies the reason why the Feds are so upset at present. I have to go now. Make sure you don't go any place where we can't keep in touch with you. You're in heaps of danger, believe me.' The police officer climbed to the base of the Tree of Knowledge.

John slowly went back to the *Shakespeare* and slept fitfully as his brain pondered where on earth in this little place would be the reason for all this turmoil which was putting his life in danger.

The next morning he just wanted to relax. Grabbing a heritage-tourism leaflet from the hotel reception, he picked out a couple of interesting places to visit. Across from the hotel was the old picture theatre. It was in art deco style with old canvas seats still being used. It served as a radio station now with pictures still on a Friday night.

Later, strolling along the street opposite the heritage-listed railway station, John drank a much needed cup of coffee in a nearby cafe. He thought about what intrigue the old town would have been through with the striking shearers marching through the town 120 years ago. The cafe owner was not a local but a tall Nigerian who knew how to run a business. The little cafe was full of chattering

Grey Nomads and locals having their daily fix. The Nigerian's beaming smile showed off his glistening white teeth which contrasted with his black skin and curly hair.

After savouring his flat white in the Wild West town of Barcaldine, John headed off in the direction of the Masonic temple which got a good write-up in the local tourist leaflet. John had been to the Ann St Mason Temple in Brisbane so he was aware of the ritual and regalia that was associated with this ancient brotherhood. Public opinion knew the Masons as a secret society, but John doubted it was so secret, as everybody knew it existed. Instead, John reasoned, it was a society that had secrets. *Surely the Masonic movement is not involved in the present political power struggle that he was investigating,* he thought to himself.

Walking in the warm winter sunshine was pleasant especially as the roads were so wide and free of traffic. John took in the smell of the green leaves on the trees and the scent of flowers in gardens watered by the plentiful supply of artesian bore water. The year-long floods had helped replenish the underground supply of bore water which in recent years had been depleted due to a long drought.

The Masonic temple came into view. It looked very ordinary side-on. It was just external corrugated iron cladding in a bare allotment. The usual lack of windows on the ground floor which gave the notion of secrecy was fuel for rumours. Myths of billy-goat riding and human sacrifice were the most outlandish.

When John went round to the front facade, his heart missed a beat. The beautiful decoration and painting in varied colours looked magnificent. Here in the birth place of organised political labour was this facade which rivalled the mighty pharaohs. John just had to get inside and see what lay behind this classical facade. The leaflet had indicated that a tour was available daily after lunch to see the interior. He could not wait that long. Striding up to the front entrance he assumed it would be locked but surprise, surprise, the door was ajar. He crept in and viewed the interior.

He was in the bush but the timber and high ceiling of this building were beautiful. *Who paid for all of this?* he mused. *Maybe they bet on the billy-goat rides,* he chuckled to himself.

Once through the door, he heard voices coming from the main hall. He crept closer and made out a group of tourists being given a tour by a guide. No wonder the door was ajar. John's eyes took in the vast wooden ceiling which had star-like signs pointing to the floor. The room had all the regalia and insignias of the Masons.

His eyes gazed upwards again but not for long as a shot rang out and the echo kept vibrating against the tin walls. He hit the floor in a flash. At the same time an arm grabbed him by the shoulder and an exasperated voice thundered, 'you will get us all killed, if you keep being a pain of a journalist.'

After being scared by a policeman in the bowels of the Tree of Knowledge and enduring gunshots at the Comet Masonic Temple, John was beginning to feel that he had better go to somewhere a bit quieter. He might be an investigative journalist but he did not expect to be involved in all this "cloak and dagger" stuff. *It does not do the blood pressure any good either*, he mused.

After packing his gear, he left the rambling old-world hospitality of the Shakespeare Hotel in Barcaldine, hired a four-wheel-drive and headed to Winton. That would be quieter.

Winton had only the Waltzing Matilda Centre and old dinosaur relics as tourist attractions. *I can catch up on my story there and not be followed by the boys from the Federal Police who seem to think I am in some kind of danger. How could I possibly be in danger in these small Outback towns?* John's mind was rationalizing the fact that he could never be in danger even if he was involved in a political minefield. The Feds would say he was in denial, because he *was* in danger.

He enjoyed driving the main highway to Winton over the long straight stretches of road, expanding into a ribbon reaching to the far horizon. No one was going to take a pot shot when he was on this highway. There was some danger to life and limb when a huge road train full of cattle heading to Townsville for live shipment overseas was passing him in the opposite direction. The slipstream made his 4WD rock and shudder and he hung onto the steering wheel tightly. He stopped briefly in Ilfracombe, an old former mining town, and Longreach, a busy bustling regional centre.

He passed the Stockman's Hall of Fame where modern architecture clashed with the brown bush grass surrounding it. Nearby the QANTAS display of its first Boeing 747 jet loomed up and he drove past.

John reached the outskirts of Winton later that day and headed for a drink in one of the old-style wooden hotels that lined the main street. It was pleasantly warm as he slumped down into a cane chair close to the footpath and surveyed the street, especially the store opposite which housed a world famous dinosaur collection.

A tall elderly Aboriginal stockman came out of a bar and remarked, 'The place might look quiet to a city boy like you but the Mafia would find this place too hot for them. Just be careful, that is my advice.'

John, smiling weakly, thought to himself, *what would this silly old black fellow know anyway*? The spurned advice would turn out to more accurate than John could ever imagine.

After quenching his thirst, John crossed the wide main street and entered a building, which was a former hardware store. Tall ceilings towered over lots of tongue and groove used in the building. He began to feel a little cautious – the same feeling he had when the shots rang out during the visit to the Masonic hall, in Barcaldine.

Now shaded from the glare of the western sun, John moved around the darkened exhibits brightened by a few light bulbs hanging from the roof. He was fascinated with all the memorabilia that was on display showing how the early pioneers lived in this harsh environment. Dinosaurs roamed the plains of Australia before the Ice Age wreaked havoc and they could not survive. However, fossils told their story. The exhibits contained some huge dinosaur feet. Moving slowly to the back of the museum, he sensed he was being followed. *Not that police officer again*, John thought.

Looking up he saw a large sign indicating the way to the reconstruction of the largest dinosaur remains found in Australia. This excited his curiosity and he followed the directions to the back of the building. There, in a huge glass case, was a reconstruction of this 10m high dinosaur, which roamed the continent over 100 million years ago. Known as Saurapod, this breed of dinosaur devoured smaller dinosaurs as well as other prey.

This Saurapod in the museum had such a realistic body and head. The dinosaur's eyes were like those of the *Mona Lisa* painting in the Louvre, Paris. John moved, and eyes kept their gaze on him. He was sure the head moved as well. *It must be the light playing tricks on my senses*, John thought. He moved back and took out his camera to record this strange behaviour of the fake dinosaur. Fiddling with his Canon SLR, he started to look through the viewfinder to a good angle of the head and eyes staring at him. He pressed the action button and expected a small explosion of light from camera flashlight system, which never came. Instead, two parallel beams of light shot out from the Saurapod's eyes and singed his hair. At the same time, the glass in the cage shattered and the wood in the floor burned and smelt of carbon as the flashes embedded into the museum floor.

He gasped, not believing his eyes and fell heavily on the floor.

A voice in a slow drawl spoke to him in an I-told-you sort of way. 'I said be careful, some people do not like you'. The tall frame of the Aboriginal stockman bent down and picked John up from the charred floor.

'Thanks mate,' John weakly uttered as he brushed the dust and ashes off his jeans. He knew that he was on to something politically big but realized that he would never be able to produce a story his editor would accept without being sued for millions. No hard evidence, no video clips and no willing witnesses to any of the events he had experienced. The harshness of the outback, the birthplace of militant unions and equally competitive employers, and the brotherhood of the Masons embracing both sides ensured secrecy would remain. The Aussie tradition of "mateship" was stronger than ever in the vastness of the bush.

The Qantas Link plane took off from Barcaldine the following day with John aboard. It never arrived in Brisbane.

A committee of enquiry was set up to determine what happened. The wreckage was never found.

The Australian Labor Government, the trade unions and the mining industry, are still opposed by the Greens Party. The Indigenous leaders are at logger heads with everyone. The populist Bob Katter Australia Party and Clive Palmer United Party could be, according to the polls, heading for the balance of power at the Federal election later that year. Unlike John, these problems would not disappear at the ballot box.

A FARMER'S LOVE
Bakthi Ross

A trail of cracked mud.
No water, no sheep.
Birds flew away long before the drought set in.
A dusty boot stamping on the ground.

A few dry twigs here and there.
A dame at the veranda wiping her sweaty face.
A dog curled up sleeping and given up hope.

A day dream is the only thing keeping them going.
If they were birds they would have sensed the
Long lasting drought and flown away north.

Now without wings,
And without hope.
Just sitting and staring at the dust flying up
And down on their land

Dusk is the only time of a few smiles and a few conversations
Between the dame and the man.
She cooked that frozen corn and peas,
Only green to be seen for miles.

A few glasses of beer'll do him til morning.
No dreams or worries will wake him up,
After that cold beer.

Dawn was like noon,
Started with a scorching heat.
Her man with his dusty boots,
Went around kicking dirt.
He was back on the porch before you know,
Covering his face with an akubra.

No point in looking at the dusty land.
He covered his face and crossed his legs and went to sleep.
Months went by,
Not a cloud to be seen.

Then a sudden loud thunder woke him up.
Black clouds moved faster than water,
Covered the whole sky.
At first a few drops of water,
Fell between his dusty boots.
Then the rain turned the land into a muddy pool.

The dame and the man stood there in the rain,
Got themselves all wet.
A childish fun between them,
Showered the hope of happiness.

A few days went by,
A green leaf and a new grass,
The man was back at dawn to work on the farm.
Now his sweat is dust free,
And shines like the smiling green leaves.

Serendipity! A farmer's love was born

PLAUSIBLE DENIABILITY

Raelene Purtill

OLIVIA Kent stood in the back garden of her beach house allowing the rhythm of the morning tide to move into her wakening. The cup of English-Breakfast tea she enjoyed each day at this time was comforting. Holding it firmly in both hands, she lifted her eyes to the horizon. A large container ship made its way out to sea. She vaguely wondered where it was headed, before bringing her gaze closer to shore. A dozen early morning swimmers and surfers bobbed above the breakers. A lone fisherman baited the hook at the tip of his surf rod.

Movement at the bottom of the garden brought her attention to the wooden stairs leading to the beach. She looked down and smiled as Nick arrived home from his morning run. The presence of her adult nephew warmed her heart. She could not love him more if he had been her own. That was not to be, so there was Nick.

'Good morning, Aunt Lily.' He had called her Lily since he was a toddler – his version of the truncation Livy. She still found it sweet. He applied a generous kiss to her cheek. When her response was a sharp intake of breath and a frown of pain, he stopped with concern and observed his aunt more fully.

'What's this?'

'It's nothing.'

'Lily, you're hurt. Let me see.'

She had tried to hide a red jagged scratch and a deep purple bruise under a light scarf about her neck.

'What on earth happened?'

'Couldn't sleep. Fell over in the dark.'

'No, you did not. I would have heard you. You know that.'

Olivia closed her eyes. *Please don't interrogate me, Nick,* she thought. *I can't tell you what happened. You cannot know that part of my life.*

'Come with me,' he said.

He led her back through the house where he sat her down at the large kitchen table and proceeded to tend her wounds. She winced at his ministrations but the resolve to keep her secret and not reveal the cause of her injuries remained steady.

'Many on the beach?'

'Oh, the usual faithful,' he replied. 'And don't change the subject.'

'Subject? I wasn't aware we were discussing anything in particular.'

'You know what I mean.'

Olivia sighed, replaced the scarf and returned her silver hair to its usual bun at the nape of her now bandaged neck. 'I need to get on with some writing, dear. Charles will be here at the end of the week.'

'That editor of yours...' Nick left the sentence unfinished and shook his head.

Olivia smiled. Nick was so protective of her. *Perhaps my secret would be safe with him?* 'Charles is my boss,' she said aloud, with a shrug that pulled at her injury.

'He doesn't only edit your stories. He's controlling your life.'

'Not as much as he thinks, Nick.'

There had always been animosity between Nick and Charles. Nick saw in him a leech of a man who had over-stepped the boundaries of his role as Olivia's editor. He thought he could appear at the beach house any time of the day or night. He sucked the life out of Aunt Olivia. She had desired a carefree creative existence as a romance novelist but instead she bled pages for Charles Baxter like a slave. Charles viewed Nick with suspicion: a healthy, admittedly handsome, twenty-eight-year-old man living with a vulnerable middle-aged lady at a secluded beach house. He should be making use of the education for which she had paid. He should be living in the suburbs with a pretty wife and the obligatory children. Charles wondered what Nick was thinking, living off his aunt as he did. Olivia herself knew neither of them had the control of her life they believed they did. Neither knew her secret.

Olivia sat at her desk by the window now watching the ocean. The container ship had disappeared from view. The swimmers and surfers were beginning to leave the beach and Nick was in the shower.

She turned back to the computer scanning the last paragraph she had written. The screen underneath it remained blank but for the flashing cursor. Blinking, waiting. Her neck began an aching throb. The words that usually spilled from her were stuck on their journey from her brain to her typing fingers because of this unfortunate injury at her neck. She returned her gaze to the blue ocean, golden sand, cotton ball clouds, green lawn and her pink hibiscus.

The colours beckoned. She rose.

'I'm going for a walk,' she called at Nick's door.

On the beach, Olivia relished the sensation of the waves and sand at her feet. She faced the warm sun and drew her neck back as much as she could before the pain restrained her.

'Dumb. Dumb. Stupid mistake,' she muttered to herself.

Last night's job was supposed to be simple. It was the launch party for Angela Connolly's new crime novel, the plot involving a diamond necklace. The real thing was on loan from Harrods Jewellers for the event. When Tony had learned Olivia would be there, he could not resist.

'C'mon baby, you can do it.'

'Tony, I'll be a guest. How can I lift it without getting caught?'

'Never stopped you before. You'll work something out.'

Until yesterday her life as a novelist and her life as a criminal had been entirely separate. Last night they had collided violently. Angela's novel itself had presented the answer to Tony's request. There, in its extensive pages, was the clue to pulling off this little job. Angela's words had described the necklace in detail as the author had studied the one in Harrods. Tony's counterfeiters set about making the duplicate Olivia had secreted in her shimmering clutch purse.

She slid in and out of the crowd comfortably as the matriarch of Baxter's Publishing House. Most knew her well and greeted her warmly. She made the expected salutations to the guest of honour and moved back to the glass case containing the prize. While her story lines were usually well plotted, her jobs for Tony were somewhat vague in their execution. She would know when the moment came; the time at which she would procure the necklace and leave the duplicate in its place. That moment would reveal itself very soon. She could feel it.

A steward passed her with a tray of appetizers. There were tragic little prunes wrapped in bacon and pierced together with a toothpick, green gherkins and pale cheese embracing on their cracker bed and king prawns bowing in reverence to Lord Lettuce. As her literary eye surveyed the tray of delicacies, the boy tripped over her foot.

The moment not only arrived, it announced itself with squeals of surprise, peals of broken glass and the thud of an embarrassed waiter at her feet. Olivia dove at the cabinet. When her neck and the side of the cabinet connected, she thought she must have miscalculated but as she slid to the floor, switching necklaces deftly through the shattered glass, she realised her way had been obstructed by an errant prune that had escaped its bacon captor.

In the chaos, her deed was not detected. The real necklace was safe in her purse, but, oh God, her neck hurt. She lay prone listening to the sounds of salvage and disarray around her.

'Madam, you're bleeding,' said a low voice from above. Instinctively she tightened the grip on her purse and then took the warm hand. She rose to look into the soft concern on the face of...

...her hero.

That's it!

Olivia made her middle-aged way back up the beach, pumping ideas giving her legs their momentum.

When Nick looked in on Aunt Lily that afternoon, she was tapping her keyboard enthusiastically and thoroughly.

Silently, he collected the knuckle-duster, gun and balaclava from beneath the floor of the cupboard under the stairs, stashed them in a worn sports bag and closed the front door of the beach house without disturbing her.

FEET OF CLAY
Long John Best

*When I was young, everything seemed black and white but the years have
taught me to compromise and make allowances for both myself and for
others. One thing you can't compromise on is death. If you're not here you
can't fix things. Give yourself some slack, being here for someone is what
counts.* – **LJB.**

Role models, aren't they hard to find, someone who's kind and true,
Or does someone, strong and silent, have more appeal to you?
No matter what your preference, I think it's fair to say,
That everyone I looked up to revealed they'd feet of clay.

But did that depress me? Never; it just served to advance
My theory, that, while you're alive, you get another chance
To prove yourself; so have a go, and with luck, some kid might say,
'You've taught me everything I know, and I love you, Feet of Clay.

Oh, I went through all them phases: cheating, lying, gambling, beer,
But don't tell me that's what life's about, the reason we are here.
No, what I'm trying to tell you, and not coping all that well,
Is that life does have its highs and lows, its heaven and its hell.

But while ever you are breathing, then you get another chance,
To see your Grandkids born and grow, and laugh and sing and dance.
So hang in there mate, like I did, and who knows, maybe they'll say,
'You've taught us everything we know, and we love you, Feet of Clay.

BEWARE OF THE COLEMANS

Maurice Hardy

TARA was stunned. She could not believe it. Since her early childhood one thing frequently entered her imagination, sometimes triggering nightmares. Today it was right in front of her.

She thought of the sayings that she and many local children became familiar with: 'Be good or old Ma Coleman will get you.' 'Don't wander off alone or Old Ma will grab you.' 'Old Ma Coleman takes naughty kids back to her bush shack, cooks them and feeds them to her boys.' They were told her boys were not really boys at all, but half men and half monsters. For parents, it proved an effective disciplinary tool.

When she first saw the old VW van, Tara was unconcerned. Like most people of the district, she knew it belonged to Roy – the only Coleman who regularly came to town. Bushy-bearded Roy was a man of few words. He worked at the local sawmill, picked up supplies and managed any business on behalf of the family, but basically kept to himself. Today however Tara knew the old lady standing near Roy's van must be Old Ma Coleman. As Roy brought items from the supermarket, Old Ma packed them inside the van.

Continuing to watch, Tara saw a passing couple experience Old Ma's wrath.

'Stop ya gawkin'. Git away,' she screeched, before bashing the side of the van with her walking stick. Visibly embarrassed, the pair hurried away.

Roy returned with more groceries before heading towards the hardware store. As Old Ma picked up one bag, the bottom split, spilling its contents. Most items settled in the gutter, except a can of peaches. It rolled down the street before coming to rest – at Tara's feet.

An irrational inexplicable fear engulfed her. Every instinct told her to get out of there. But she could not. Reaching down, she picked up the can. Taking a deep breath she started towards the van, aware of Old Ma's eyes burning into her as she approached. Tara could not bring herself to look at the old lady, preferring to stare at the road until the edge of the vehicle entered her vision.

She raised her head and met Old Ma's eyes. The wrinkles, scars and lines portrayed a tough and basic life. Old Ma's eyes showed suspicion; as well as understanding, or a strange intelligence; something Tara could not define. Hastily handing over the can, Tara kneeled and gathered the remaining items.

'Thank you, child,' muttered the old lady. 'Ya have a good soul.'

Tara tried to reply but the words would not come. She simply smiled and nodded.

'Be warned, child. Bad things are comin'. Big storms...Stock up with plenty of tucker 'n' stuff. Git to somewhere safe 'n' stay there.'

'Remember what I say child; now git.' The change of tone took Tara by surprise. Feeling like a chastised child, she turned and almost broke into a run returning to her car.

____ooo____

'HEY look Harry, it's Meagan,' called the excited Helen McKenzie. She was at the farmhouse window after hearing a car drive up. Putting down his coffee, Harry dashed to the front door to greet his favourite daughter. Meagan was standing on the lawn taking in the view when her parents joined her. Having grown up here, she truly loved the place.

'What a pleasant surprise. Why didn't you tell us you were coming?' asked Helen, after hugs and kisses were exchanged.

'Work related, I'm afraid,' replied the attractive brunette. 'Part of my job as the new Field Operations Manager is to visit our stations, check and install new equipment and train staff.

'Yeah, you've landed a top job there,' said Harry. 'With the Bureau of Meteorology you can't go wrong. You'll be running the place in no time.'

Meagan smiled.

'Actually a major weather event is predicted to develop over the next few days. The remnants of tropical cyclone Angus combined with a blast of upper-level Antarctic air will produce a severe storm cell off Tasmania's West Coast.

'There's even a theory an increase of solar flare activity could influence the system. I'm here to collect and analyse data and coordinate with Hobart HQ.'

Harry laughed. 'I've heard the lot...solar flares; what a joke. How could they possibly affect weather patterns on earth?'

'You'd be surprised, Dad,' answered Meagan, although she could not conceal a slight grin.

'Anyway your work sounds important to me. Come in, dear, I'll put the kettle on,' said Helen.

'Thanks Mum. Would you mind if I stayed for a few days? Based here I can access Cape Grim Station and monitor readings from our remote sites.'

'You are always welcome Meagan. Your room is as you left it.'

With Harry's assistance, Meagan carried her gear into the house.

She chose to set up her electronic equipment in her favourite place; a corner by the lounge-room window. From here the view was spectacular.

Yes, Meagan thought. *It's great to be home.*

The three spent the next two hours catching up on all the news, laughing and reminiscing. 'Where's Tara?' asked Meagan as the conversation paused.

'In town as far as I know,' replied Harry. 'Don't know what will become of that girl. She needs a few lessons from you.'

'But isn't she leaving for uni next week?' continued Meagan.

Meagan could sense a change in Harry's mood.

'She'd better be, but I wouldn't guarantee it. She would prefer to ride horses and do farm work. And there's another problem – Sean Cooper; bloody no-hoper, just like his father.'

'Come on dad, Sean and Tara have been friends since primary school, they grew up together.'

'Kids are different. She's a young woman and should act like one. There is no way any daughter of mine is going to throw her future away over a moron like Sean Cooper. She knows how I feel and Cooper knows what to expect if I find him anywhere near her. Anyway, time to milk the cows. You coming, Helen?'

____ooo____

FOR Meagan it was a long night. Sleep was intermittent and she lost count of the times she woke. At 1am, she heard Tara come home, and, at five, her parents leave for the morning milking. Eager to commence her monitoring tasks, Meagan showered and, with her coffee and bowl of cereal, settled at her computer.

An arm draped over her shoulder and she felt a kiss on her cheek. 'Good morning little sister,' Meagan said.

'Hi Megs. This looks complicated,' said Tara, glancing at the screen. Meagan began an explanation but, realising it was not registering with her sister, she gave up.

'Looking forward to uni?'

Emotion surfaced in Tara's voice. 'No...I don't want to go. I'd hate living in Hobart. Farm work is in my blood; it's all I've ever wanted to do.'

'Hey, you'll be fine. Once you settle in, you'll love it.'

'No. I belong here with Sean. We love each other so much. Dad is such a bully. He doesn't understand. You know what he's like; it's his way or no way.'

'That's a bit unfair, Tara. He only wants the best for your future and career.'

'Come on Megs, you're his favourite; you've never had to put up with his raving like I have.'

'Hey don't be like that,' Meagan stood and gave her sibling a hug.

'Don't worry, Megs. I'll go to uni; I don't have much choice. But between you and me, I'm meeting Sean tonight to discuss our options; he may be able to get a job in Hobart. Whatever, we plan to say goodbye our own way.' Tara left for the kitchen, leaving Meagan to her thoughts.

____ooo____

APART from a modest dwelling, truck driver/mechanic Jim Cooper's property included numerous workshops and sheds.

Perfect, thought Tara, as she parked her car inside a disused garage. Moments later she was climbing in beside Sean Cooper as his 4X4 wagon roared to life. The sandy-haired larrikin gave her a kiss and soon they were heading up a bush track towards their special place; Dawson's Bluff.

Although the trail was steep and full of pot holes, Tara felt relaxed. She and Sean had made the journey many times. Reaching the top, Sean crossed the clearing and parked near the tree line. Normally the view was breathtaking, but today's overcast conditions diminished its impact.

With the seats laid back, Tara wrapped her arms around Sean's neck, drawing him closer. Passionately they kissed.

'What are we going to do?' he whispered. 'I can't bear the thought of you going away.'

'We'll think of something. Dad is such a pig.'

'I don't know what else to do, Tara. I've worked for him when he's been stuck for a farmhand; mostly for nothing. I've picked up stuff from town for him, but still he treats me like dirt.'

'It's not you, Sweetie. One day we'll be together, I promise,' Tara could feel tears welling in her eyes.

'I love you,' replied Sean.

_____ooo_____

EVEN with the grainy SKYPE image on her screen, Meagan could see alarm in his face. From Cape Grim Research Station, Ross Long's report was unnerving.

'This thing will be bad, Meagan. In the past four hours we've measured wind gusts over 100kmh. The rain, thunder and lightning are incredible; hear it?'

'I certainly can Ross. You'd better get them to shut down the wind turbines. From our reports the Bureau issued a State-wide extreme weather alert. Police and emergency services are on standby; I'm in constant contact. We expect the north-west and particularly the Circular Head region to be impacted most.'

'Jesus Meagan, there's going to be some damage before this is over. What's the latest wave-rider buoy reading?'

'Would you believe twenty one metres and increasing? Better go Ross, be in touch; stay safe.'

Startled by the exchange, Helen and Harry approached their daughter.

'What can we expect here?' asked Harry.

'Well Dad, you heard Ross. I suggest you secure any loose items, put vehicles under cover and get livestock to the open paddocks.'

Harry hurried outside, leaving mother and daughter amid the beeping electronic equipment and radio bulletins.

_____ooo_____

OPENING her eyes, Tara realised she had dozed off. A glance at Sean confirmed he had too. The rocking and swaying of the vehicle had awoken them. Tara felt a wave of panic. Outside, the scene had turned chaotic. The moderate westerly blowing when they arrived had turned gale force, slamming into their vehicle. Nearby trees thrashed violently.

'This is scary Sean; let's go.'

'Sure thing, babe. It's come from nowhere,' yelled Sean.

'Megs was trying to warn me; wish I'd taken more notice.'

Sean's attempt to start the motor resulted in a clicking sound.

'Oh shit, no. The battery's flat.'

Simultaneously a vicious lightning flash and torrential rain erupted, followed by booming thunder. Sean tried the ignition again, same result.

The next lightning strike seemed to 'fizz' through the sky and the associated thunder clap was the loudest yet. To their right, a huge pine tree exploded into a ball of fire. Branches and debris rained down. Tara heard an almighty creaking sound but had no time to react as the massive bough fell across their vehicle.

_____ooo_____

'WHAT was that?' Someone's at the door,' exclaimed Helen McKenzie. She returned, accompanied by a distressed saturated Jan Cooper, their neighbour.

'Oh God it was terrible,' sobbed Jan. 'The roof of our house peeled off. We thought we'd be safe in Jim's workshop, but the side wall caved in. He's pinned under a steel girder...our phone's not working...I didn't know who else to turn to.'

'Typical of Jim Cooper,' said Harry. 'Always cutting corners; this was bound to happen sooner or later.'

Helen was ropeable.

'Forget your stupid feud, Harry McKenzie. These people are our neighbours and need our help.'

Seeing Meagan was equally as appalled, Harry relented.

'Look I'm sorry. I'll go straight over.'

'I'm coming too, Dad,' said Meagan. 'I'm a qualified first-aid officer. Our phone is out as well so I'll call an ambulance via my satellite link.'

'Thank you. But please hurry...Jim's in a bad way,' replied Jan.

It was a short distance to the Cooper home but Meagan could never remember travelling in worse conditions. Poor visibility and wind velocity forced Harry to continually fight to control his vehicle.

They arrived to find the entire house collapsed. Household items and furniture were strewn about like toys; transformed into potential missiles. Struggling through the turbulence, Meagan was relieved when they entered the workshop. Although the far wall and western corner had caved in, the remaining structure offered some protection from the elements.

Jim was semi conscience and in the early stages of shock. The steel beam had crushed his right leg so severely a section above the knee was almost non-existent. Meagan saw a piece of bone protruding from the bloodied flesh. She shuddered and momentarily closed her eyes.

Jacking up the beam Harry was able to drag the victim free, enabling Meagan to begin cleaning and dressing the wounds.

'Jim, Jim, can you hear me mate?' asked Harry kneeling over the injured man.

'Is that you Harry? I've done it this time haven't I? Am I going to die Harry?' whispered Jim.

'Not a chance, Jim Cooper. I'd have no one to argue with.'

Jim smiled as in the distance ambulance sirens could be heard.

The medics were full of praise for Meagan's work. But as she suspected, they considered an amputation inevitable.

Back in Harry's ute, Meagan watched the ambulance disappear into pelting rain. Before they could move, a tremendous crash caught their attention. The site was surreal as an entire shed lifted off its foundations before landing in a nearby field as a twisted mess. On the original site stood a vehicle; one Harry recognised.

'That's Tara's car,' he cried.

TARA felt dazed and minutes passed before she could focus. She screamed as she saw the huge tree section between her and the driver's side of the vehicle. The impact had flattened the bonnet, roof and back of Sean's car.

'Sean, Sean, can you hear me?' she yelled.

An audible moan gave her comfort.

After several attempts, she was able to kick the door open. Racing to the other side she groaned in horror at the amount of damage. Through the crumpled door she saw Sean's blood-covered face. He was conscious.

'You've got to get help Tara. I think I'm okay, but my legs are pinned and it hurts like hell.'

'But there's nobody living within miles of here. Shit, Sean, what will I do?'

'One family does live near here, on the other side of the Bluff.'

'You mean...'

'Yes Tara, I mean the Coleman's.'

'But I can't go there. Not in this storm...' Tara burst into tears as she realised Sean had lost consciousness again.

The rain, wind, thunder and lightning combined to create a night from hell. Terrified and shaky, Tara set off on her journey to the place of her nightmares; Old Ma Coleman's home.

Her mind was racing with conflicting thoughts. She knew being under trees in a thunder storm and high winds was dangerous, but in exposed areas she could hardly stand against the wind. Each lightning flash revealed tree branches, but to Tara they looked more like giant fingers reaching for her, trying to grab her. She quickened her pace. Another flash and she saw him; a man standing in trees to her right. Utter fear engulfed her as she ran for her life. Tripping on a fallen branch she fell heavily and struck her head on a rock...the darkness came.

____ooo____

SHE awoke in a place warm and comfortable, while the aroma of freshly baked bread was like heaven. Opening her eyes, Tara found she was lying on a sofa beside a fire place. Her head wound had been bandaged and she was in dry clothing. Carrying a bowl of soup and slices of bread, an old lady approached. Tara recognised her...Old Ma Coleman.

'Here child, this'll fix ya up.'

It was a weird sensation, but hunger outweighed fear. Accepting the bowl, Tara proceeded to enjoy the most delicious broth she had ever tasted. Her attention was attracted to numerous paintings adorning the cabin walls.

'Wow, these are excellent. Who's the artist?'

'Why, they're all mine child. But I can't paint anymore; the old eyes are buggered.'

The door opened and the three Coleman boys entered. Roy was carrying someone and, as he drew closer, Tara recognised Sean.

'This bloke is bloody lucky; plenty of scratches, cuts and bruises but no broken bones. He'll be okay,' Roy said as if reading her thoughts.

'But how did you find him?' asked Tara.

'We saw the wagon up on the Bluff. With the storm comin' we knew there'd be trouble. While Billy and me went to free this fella, Byron tried to help you. But you got spooked, ran away, fell and hit your head.'

'Billy and Byron are good boys, child, but they don't talk too good,' explained Old Ma.

While the old lady treated Sean's injuries, a relieved Tara settled down on her sofa. Safe from the storm and feeling warm and contented; she fell asleep.

____ooo____

INSIDE the McKenzie homestead, Harry, Helen, Meagan and Jan Cooper heard a vehicle drive up and stop briefly before leaving. Moments later the door opened and, holding hands, Tara and Sean entered. An emotional reunion ensued and the obvious injuries were assessed.

Harry approached. Giving Sean a pat on the shoulder, he turned to his younger daughter.

'I've been thinking. Since I'm not getting any younger and don't have a son, I wonder if you would consider forgetting uni and working with me on the farm?'

Tears flowed as the father and his daughter embraced.

'Now Tara tell us; where the hell have you been?' asked Meagan.

'Um, Serendipity,' replied Tara, smiling.

MOVE OVER JAMES BOND Assignment No. 7
Vera Murray

ERNEST Moneylove, being short and slim, was desperately trying to improve his physique by attending the local gym several times a week. His unruly hair was now greased down. It caused his wide mouth to look larger and did not help his overall appearance. It fell short of being anything like James Bond in appearance. His girlfriend Estella, had heard him say many, many times, 'Move over James Bond; I'm going to be up there with you shortly.' She wished he would hurry up, as she told him she could not wait forever.

On this particular morning, Ernest, his expression serious, arrived at the Drug Squad Office ready and eager to bring another drug dealer to justice before his pushy fellow agent, John Smith, did.

He had not been seated at his desk very long before he was called into the Chief's office. He quickly tied up a loose shoelace before scrambling hastily upright, and barging into his boss's office.

His waiting chief, Mr Grant Stand, sighed and muttered, 'Why am I cursed with this bumbling daydreamer?'

'Sorry sir, I didn't hear you what you said,' spoke Ernest as he fronted the boss's desk.

'You weren't supposed to,' snapped the Chief; his narrowed eyes staring into Ernest's.

'NO, SIR.'

The boss sucked in his breath. He was silent for several moments before announcing, 'I have an assignment for you Moneylove.'

Now this one's sure to get me up there with you James, so be ready to move over.

'MONEYLOVE...to continue...John Smith was originally assigned to this investigation. However, he phoned in this morning to tell me he's gone down with a bad case of the flu. He's confined to bed and therefore unable to travel.'

What a sneak. Smithy was okay yesterday. If he's got himself out of this assignment there must be something wrong with it. I wonder what it is, but, no matter, I've got James Bond's system to follow.

'Moneylove, listen carefully. We've received information that supplies of marijuana appear to be coming from the Sunnyland fruit growing area, which is mostly scrubland. Properties there are large. Some are covered by thick growth, while others are fruit farms. Just where, and on whose property it's being grown hasn't been found. This is what you're going to find out Moneylove.'

Sunnyland...the bush. Always wanted to see the bush...now I'm going, and it'll be like a paid holiday. 'YES SIR.'

'Go now to the store downstairs and pick out a set or two of worker's clothes, and don't forget we're on a budget.'

'Yes Sir.'

Ernest backed to the door, bumping into it. Red faced, he turned and opened the door quickly. He was pleased he did not know what his boss was now muttering. He returned to his desk and prepared for his assignment. He grinned across at the closest fellow worker, Nigel, before entering the lift to go to the store below.

The following morning, Ernest, dressed in khaki work clothes, and with a backpack slung over his shoulder, boarded the train to Sunnyland. His boss had informed him which carriage to board. As he climbed in, he almost tripped over an assortment of bags lying on the floor. As he tried to regain his balance, the train jerked as it took off, and he was pitched forward. Before he could recover, a hand shot out of a nearby seat and jerked him back upright.

He turned, to find himself looking into eyes set in the plain features of a long-haired girl in tight jeans. He noted her eyes were pools of blue.... his favourite.

Not like the beauties James Bond attracts, but one has to start somewhere, and she does have beautiful eyes.

She jerked her thumb towards the vacant seat beside her. 'Sit.' It was more a command than an invitation.

Ernest obeyed. He squeezed past her and flopped into the seat beside the window.

'It's not hard to see that you're also a fruit picker going to Sunnyland.'

'Yair,' he replied.

'Your build doesn't look the best for all-day work, and I see ya gear is new...first time?'

'Sure is...but money's scarce at the moment. One has to do something to earn a crust. What about you?'

'Been to the same place before. They feed ya well there.' She stretched to make herself more comfortable, and added, 'Me name's Carol.'

'I'm Ernest...Ernest Moneylove.'

'Really?' Carol looked amused but refrained from laughing.

Ernest made no reply. He did not consider it necessary to admit to a stranger that he was an admirer and fan of James Bond, and his adopted name was in line with the people James Bond met or associated with in his films.

'What's the set up on the property?' he asked Carol.

'It's a large property, like all the others around there, but half of them seem to be completely covered in bush. It doesn't seem to bother anyone. Perhaps no one lives on them. On the Bentleys' property, there's a large house where the Douglas family live and at the back is a big shed where the fruit is sorted, packed and sent to buyers. Also, further back behind the main house is another smaller house. I believe the elderly retired Bentley couple, the real owners, live there. When the owners retired, they leased out their property to the Douglas family. On the right of the main house is the accommodation for the workers. We're not allowed to wander. You have to keep within the fenced boundary enclosing our quarters, when off duty, or the dogs'll tear you to bits.

They told us that some fences around the property are electric, but no one knows for sure. It's now gone mostly back to bush, so you wouldn't want to wander too far from the farm, anyway. You'd be completely lost.'

Eight hours later, the train pulled into Sunnyland station, much to Ernest's relief. He had fallen asleep several times, only to be shaken awake by Carol. She told him he was snoring. *I wonder if James snores...no...no...what am I thinking?*

After a two-hour bus trip, over mostly unsealed terrain, that Ernest thought would never end, they arrived at the farm.

Ernest filed out of the bus with the others and followed behind Carol to stand before the overseer, a tall man, brown of face and arms from the sun. He was called Warren. He was in the company of two dogs, Gin and Tonic. *I don't recall that James ever had to deal with two rough savage mixed-breed dogs like these* mongrels. *I'll have to make friends with them somehow if I want to search the place. Dogs love food. If I can do it without getting too much attention, I'll save some from our meals to give them. That should make them friendly towards me.*

The group followed the overseer to their living and dining quarters. At the entrance he called their names one by one. Each was given a number to match the one on their allotted sleeping area. This was followed by a meal in the dining room Ernest ate hastily, to be one of the first to reach his allocated bed. He was fast asleep seconds after climbing between the sheets.

The next morning Ernest and his fellow fruit pickers were each given a basket, which they were to fill. They were told that a truck would drive down later past them and each basket would be emptied into it. He was pleased that he and Carol were allocated the same area.

On that first day Ernest kept up with the other pickers but it soon became apparent that he would be lagging well behind them as each day passed, as his back and arms ached more and more. His basket was never full when they were emptied into the back of the truck. *I'll be having a word or two with my gym master when I get home. I should be as fit as a boxer after what I pay him.*

Ernest knew he was there to investigate, and was growing impatient. He wondered how he could leave the workers' area without being seen and questioned. *I know now why Smithy didn't take this on. I bet he suddenly got better once he knew I was sent on the job, and is back in the office. If I don't succeed I will be recalled and the Chief and Smithy will never let me forget it. But James Bond always found a way, so I will. But how can I get past the dogs? James Bond would never be afraid of two savage dogs, and neither am I. I'll have to give them more food from other plates when Warren's not looking. That'll make them even friendlier.*

The following morning he was called into the home office, which was situated beneath the highset residence. *I'm getting good at this fruit picking, so they're probably going to give me a "thank you" or maybe a bonus for my good work.* However, Ernest possessed a small fear which had crept in, and which he failed to dismiss completely from his mind. *Although unlikely, if I was sent packing, I know the Chief would transfer me to desk duties where I'd die of boredom.*

On entering the office, Ernest stood stiffly, almost at attention, before a dark-haired young man and a grey-haired older man, obviously father and son. They surveyed his narrow build, before the old man beckoned Ernest to sit on one of the chairs on the opposite side of the table. The older man rubbed his hands together as he smiled at Ernest. 'I'm Don Douglas, manager, and this is my son Lenny.'

'Pleased to meet you both,' muttered Ernest nervously.

'You haven't done this work before have you?'

'No...no,' stammered Ernest.

'We realise that, it being your first time, you're not keeping up with what we expect from our workers. However, as you're probably here because you need money, we've decided to transfer you to the packing shed. It's the large shed at the back of the house. It's off limits to the workers generally, but we'll give orders that you're permitted to go there to work. You'll be escorted there and back each day by Warren and his dogs. Are you agreeable, or should you prefer to leave the farm immediately?'

My luck's in...James's luck has rubbed off on me.

'Well?'

'Oh yes...thank you sir...thank you.'

'That's settled then. Off you go. Warren will bring you over in the morning.'

Ernest scrambled to his feet and backed out of the office still muttering, 'Thank you...thank you sirs.' The two men raised their eyes and grimaced.

At six-thirty in the morning Ernest was ready. With chop bones and pieces of discarded fat stuffed into his pockets, he joined Warren, who escorted him into the shed. Ernest found it held everything necessary for sorting and packing the fruit to send to their customers. He was allotted a place between two workers and told to copy them, as they sorted the fruit by size and colour as it moved along a conveyor belt. He noticed some of the sorted fruit was kept separate and taken into an adjoining room.

'Is that for the family and friends?' queried Ernest of the nearest worker.

'Nah...some buyers only want limited amounts so they're packed separately, in that other room over there.' He nodded towards open double doors in the far wall. 'They go into the same size boxes in there, but they're padded in the bottom so the fruit doesn't roll around and get bruised.'

'Ahhh,'muttered Ernest as he looked around the room. He had already noticed another sorting table in the room which was unused. He noted that there was enough room to sort and pack many more boxes there, and wondered why a separate room was used. *That needs investigating...might turn up something.* He tried to think how he could get into it to check it out.

During the days that followed, Ernest, now confident he had made firm friends with Gin and Tonic, decided to sneak over at night when no one was around, to investigate further. He did not believe they would lock up the place with the dogs on guard.

Shortly after nightfall, and with the usual treats for the dogs in both pockets, he crept over to the shed. He turned the door-knob, but the door remained tightly shut. Disappointed, he skirted the shed. Checking the windows he found one unlocked. He had no trouble pulling it open and climbing through. He found himself in the smaller room. He drew out his torch and swung it around.

On a long table there were sealed fruit boxes addressed to several different groups. He took out his pad and pen and jotted names down. After closer examination of a box almost filled, he tugged at the sealed padding. It came out easily and he used his penknife to cut it open. Marijuana fell out. *Jackpot! I now follow the trail, as James'd do.* He shoved handfuls of it into his pockets.

Ernest froze. He could hear heavy footsteps in the main room. *Should have closed the window...silly me.* Before he could make any attempt at hiding, the door was flung open.

The room lights were switched on.

'What are you doing here?' demanded a loud voice that he recognised as Warren's.

'Well.... well.... looking for cash sir,' stammered Ernest.

'Then what are you doing with weed spilt over the counter, and on your hands?'

'Lucky find. I won't tell. I'll keep quiet.'

Warren laughed. He loudly called for Percy who almost immediately came barging in.

Percy smirked. 'Caught him I see. You're pretty slick. The boss'll be happy. I always thought he looked a sneaky bod.'

'Gag him while I hold his arms. We can't do anything with him here, but I've got an idea.'

Ernest was about to cry out but Percy was too quick with the gag so he could only murmur his protest. Tying it tightly, Percy jerked Ernest's arms back from Warren's grip, to behind his back, and tied them. Pushed roughly, Ernest was forced to march ahead of the two men. He was pulled to a sudden stop at the side of the farm truck. With Warren's help he was thrown roughly on to its back. Gin and Tonic jumped up beside him. 'Guard him,' they were told.

The vehicle moved. Ernest's body thumped up and down on the uneven back section of the truck as it bounced over the uneven surface of the road. They were following such a narrow track that the truck at times hit and cast aside branches of trees growing on either side. The moon had risen. In its light he watched carefully to make sure he would be able to find his way out if he was dumped in the thick scrub, hopefully still alive. *Things worse than this have happened to James and he kept his cool and came out victorious. So will I, but I wish my back was not lying on top of tools, especially that axe.*

When the truck screeched to a halt, Ernest's head was flung against the side of a large metal toolbox. He groaned, but was ignored as the two men jumped out. They walked over to pull him roughly off the truck and along the ground. They let him drop beside a circular metal plate. It was set into the loose dirt on a rise in the ground.

Ernest looked around. The full moon enabled him to see beyond the spot they were at. Through the open area, extending below them were rows and rows of cultivated plants.

Marijuana! Jackpot! All I have to do now is get away. What would James do? I have to think. Before he could make any escape plans, Percy had tied some rope around his legs, while Warren dragged aside the round cylinder. A large gaping hole was revealed.

'Shove him down into the old well. We'll get the next orders from the boss.'

'He won't last too long down there anyway,' was Percy's comment.

They jerked Ernest to the edge of the hole, and shoved him almost head first into the well. Ernest closed his eyes, expecting a long fall to a far distance bottom, but he found himself in a cramped position, upside down, on a bed of damp earth. His feet almost touched the underside of the lid when they drew it back in place. He began to feel cold as the dampness of the mud soaked into his clothes. He heard a muffled voice say, 'We'll come back tomorrow and finish the job.'

At breakfast in the workers' dining room, Warren told the pickers and sorters that Moneylove had it been sleep walking, fell, and hit his head. He claimed they had taken him to the local medical centre, and his belongings would be held in storage until he returned.

Carol could not believe Ernest would wander off without mentioning his intentions, especially with the dogs on guard. She followed Warren at a distance, so as to be unnoticed by him, as he made his way to Ernest's sleeping area. She watched him gather up Ernest's belongings and leave with them.

Waiting until Warren was out of the building she walked over to Ernest's bed. She had seen Ernest put his mobile phone under his mattress, and the men had not looked there. She thought that perhaps he had left her a message on it. If not, she was certain she would be able to advise someone whose number was in the phone that Ernest was in the local hospital.

She slid her hand along beneath the mattress and was pleased when her fingers closed around the phone. She opened up his list of phone numbers and dialled the first. A response came quickly. 'Nigel here...is that you Ernest?'

'No, this is Carol, a friend of Ernest's. He's disappeared. We're told he's at the local medical centre but I don't believe it. He would not have gone wandering at night without me knowing about it. We heard nothing, and there're some savage dogs here that bark at anything.'

'When did you last see him?'

'At tea last night.'

'Okay...we'll send help...don't worry.'

'Will you let his family know?'

'Sure thing...bye.'

She pocketed the phone and left for work.

Shortly before lunch there was the sound of a helicopter flying over. Carol was surprised and could not believe it had anything to do with Ernest's disappearance. It landed on the road not far from the farm. Almost immediately several police cars skidded to a halt outside the main house. Running men from the helicopter joined them.

The leader, John Smith, led the group, giving several men instructions to circle the house, and others to disappear around the back, cutting off anyone who might decide to leave. The remaining men were to stay with him.

As John Smith had his foot on the first step of the house, two dogs raced forward. One gripped his leg. He had difficult holding back a cry of pain as blood spurted. Warren appeared from inside the house. He called the dogs off. They retreated, still snarling.

'They should be tied up, the damn things,' Smithy said.

Warren tapped his leg and the dogs flopped on the ground beside him.

'Perhaps that can wait, continued Smithy. 'To get to the business on hand. This is a drug squad raid, and we're seeking one of our members. His name is Ernest Moneylove. Do you know where he is?'

Warren froze but quickly recovered. 'I believe he fled. The work was not to his liking it seems. As he was a lousy worker he won't be missed.'

'True, but there's only one problem. He wouldn't have left without advising us, as he gives us an hour-by-hour coverage of information, relative or not. We've checked the medical centre. He never turned up there. So where is he? Would you like to tell us?'

'Dunno,' Warren shrugged.

Smithy turned to his men. 'Two of you go in and search the house.' Two constables disappeared inside, while another two remained with him.

A shout came from behind the second house. Smith, limping, beside his two assistants, hurried in answer to the call. One officer walked behind Warren and pushed him on when he tried to stop.

They joined the constables now standing at the entrance to a track leading into dense bush. The two dogs kept with them.

One constable said, 'There are fresh car tracks going up there into the bush.' Smith looked to where the junior officer was pointing and agreed. Turning his gaze towards Warren's work truck, Smith said, 'I take it that's working.'

Warren nodded.

'Then you can drive us down the road and we'll see what we can find.'

Warren shrugged and climbed into the driver's seat. The dogs jumped into the back.

As they moved slowly forward Smith's two assistants kept calling out Moneylove's name. There was no answer and nothing unusual was sighted.

They eventually came to a clearing, surrounded by bush less dense than what they had already driven through.

'Stop the truck here,' commanded Smith.

Warren obliged and stopped the truck.

The men circled a small shed between two tall trees. Together they kicked in a door. Inside were only tools.

'You must have a good reason for keeping tools handy in the bush. Can you give us an explanation?' Smith asked Warren.

Before he could get a response, an officer still standing on the back of the truck spoke up, 'I can answer that. I can see between the trees from up here. There's rows and rows of what look like marijuana crops. They're growing between gaps in the bush, that wouldn't be visible from the air.'

'Jackpot!' John Smith waved his clenched fists in the air, and continued, 'Poor old Ernest. He's obviously not around here anywhere. We'll send in more searchers tomorrow. But, before we leave, tell Constable Duffield to bring over the camera.'

Constable Duffield jumped from the truck. He walked around the small clearing with camera in hand. Gin and Tonic scampered past him. They began scratching on a round metal cylinder not far from the constable's feet. He could hear a sound coming from under it.

'There's something under here. I can hear a thumping sound.' There was excitement in his voice.

'Probably snakes or a hare. I'd leave it alone. If you're finished we'll be out of here,' was Smithy's comment. Smithy's offsiders ignored him and dragged the lid away, revealing a pair of muddy shoes with their soles facing upwards.

Smithy shrugged, and walked over to look into the hole. 'Well, if it isn't me mate Ernest, loafing on the job as usual. You don't seem to do anything in a proper drug-squad manner.' He stepped back, as an officer dragged Ernest out.

As Ernest was being pulled to his feet and the ties cut off, he spat out the now loosened gag. To the annoyance of his helpers, the two dogs began to jump up on him as if delighted to see him.

John Smith, stepping quickly back to be away from the dogs, remarked, 'You look handsome with all that mud over you, but Ernest, you stink to high heaven. Those dogs can't just like your...err, good looks, so what am I missing?'

Ernest reached into his pockets and pulled out the now smelly chops. 'Only a few bones in me pockets,' was his reply. He tossed them to the excited dogs which began chewing hungrily on them.

'I've now seen you at your best,' Smith said sarcastically. 'Anyway, the boss'll be pleased he hasn't got to order a funeral for you – thanks to me. I don't think you really appreciate what a good friend I am to you. The boss'll show *his* appreciation again to me...perhaps it could turn out to be a fatter pay packet.'

Ernest could only think his response. *'You're always claiming credit for all my work. One day you'll meet your match. But this time, with Carol's help...nice Carol...I'll be able to get credit. Then Smithy, you'll be more jealous than ever.'*

He let the disturbing thoughts vanish as his eyes moved over the view. They alighted on the top of a distant mountain. *When I'm up there with you James, at the top of the game, I'll sack Smithy, and without holiday pay.*

Ernest was called to stand near where he was found so photos could be made for evidence. He tried to brush the mud from his body and clothes, but it had dried and could not be shaken off. *James never got looking like this that I know of.* The drying dirt and the odour of decaying meat together, caused Smith to insist that Ernest return to the house on the back of the truck with the dogs.

At the main house Carol was waiting. She gave Ernest a slow hug. Ernest's wide mouth was smiling even more broadly when Carol gave him a second hug. As she pulled away she pushed a piece of paper into his hand.

'My phone number's on it. Ring me sometime.'

'I sure will.'

They left the property, with Carol waving and the others watching on.

The following morning, Ernest, clean and keen, fronted up at his work place. He had already forwarded his report to his boss by messenger. More arrests were in the process of being carried out, while the marijuana crops were being destroyed.

I know Smithy would have visited the boss immediately. I bet he limped more to get sympathy. I wouldn't put that past him to have got sick leave for the dog bite. If the boss could give out knighthoods he'd give one to Smithy. But the boss'll have Carol's report by now, and it's very favourable to me. The boss will think up something to not give me a raise, but I don't care, 'cos the raise I want is to float up to the top and stand beside James Bond. Maybe he'll move aside so I can have the top spot.

Nigel greeted Ernest with a grin on his face. 'You're in for a shock.'

'What?' Ernest felt nervous. *Has Smithy done something sneaky AGAIN, to my detriment?* He drew his attention back to Nigel who was still speaking in a smug manner. 'That's for me to know and you to find out.' There was a low giggle from another close-by staff member.

Tossing his head in the air Ernest walked away. He knocked on the chief's office door.

Inside he was aghast. There was a strange man sitting in the boss's chair.

The man stood up. He waved a hand towards the chair opposite before reseating himself. 'You must be Ernest. I'm Goodberry Smartway, your new Chief.

In amazement Ernest stumbled, kicking the leg of the chair in his attempt to sit down. Finally seated, and rubbing his knee, his mouth remained slightly open.

'I can see from your expression, you didn't know that Mr Grant Stand has moved on to another government position, following what seemed to be a nervous collapse. We don't know whether it's a temporary or permanent transfer.'

Ernest wondered if his ordeal had somehow affected his hearing, but Mr Smartway's presence alone, made him believe it must be true. A feeling of relief and lightness crept over him. After a few moments he was relaxed enough to dare ask hopefully. 'And John Smith? He's not in the office.'

'John Smith's on sick leave, recovering from a badly infected leg, caused by a dog bite, I believe. He's applied for a transfer to the same section Mr Stand's new section. That's being processed now. If and when it does, and I'm sure it will, it means you'll be our top agent. I've been going through your service record and am amazed at your courage.'

Ernest wanted to say, 'James Bond has taught me to be fearless in the face of evil,' but managed to keep it to himself, feeling it could wait.

'I have also recommended a rise in your pay...not a big one...but one nevertheless.'

Ernest felt faint. *James, maybe you should move aside right now.*

'Are you all right? You seem distracted. After your ordeal, perhaps you should have a day or two off. Go now and put in a request. It'll be granted.'

Ernest mumbled, 'Thank you.' He managed to almost trip over his own feet as he pushed himself out of the chair. He was still stumbling as he left his work place.

I'm going home. Won't Estella be pleased. She keeps reminding me that her patience is nearly exhausted, but I'm sure she'll be happy to have a drink with me, or perhaps two – shaken, not stirred, just like Bond, James Bond.

SECRETS UNCOVERED
Sharyn Hutchinson

WHY did this always happen? Jessica could never find the right coloured lipstick when she was in a hurry to go out. Gary was picking her up in twenty minutes, and yet there she was standing in her bedroom, still in her underwear, with wet hair dripping on the carpet. Clothes were strewn around the room, because of course she had tried everything on, and nothing looked right. They were only going to the movies but she wanted to look nice.

The red dress was too dressy. The green dress had been just perfect, until Jessica noticed a rip in the back of it. Then she had suddenly remembered her new pink lipstick, so if she could only find where she had put that, then she would wear something to match it. The drawer in her bathroom was emptied. No new pink lipstick.

Jessica stomped her foot in frustration. She was tempted to scream and jump up and down on the spot but seeing as she was almost twenty-five (in a couple of weeks) she thought perhaps it was time to grow up.

Or not. Arrrrgghhh! Where was that lipstick? There, that felt much better – too bad if she was turning twenty-five.

Jessica was thankful that she was living alone in the house. Her Mother would have been mortified to see the current state of her bedroom and her dear sweet Grandmother would have grown some more grey hairs upon hearing the disgruntled shriek that Jessica had just bellowed out.

Jessica's Granny had moved to a retirement home, two weeks earlier, and it had been her idea for Jessica to come and live in her big old home – rent free, of course, in return for looking after Cuckoo the cockatoo, not permitted to live with his mistress in the retirement home.

Jessica had been thrilled at the idea. She was sad that Granny had finally succumbed to the pressures of maintaining such a huge old house by herself and felt the need to move. However she loved Cuckoo, who was as old as she was and she adored Granny's three-storey villa, which had been in the family for three generations. The house sat proudly and majestically on the top of a hill, overlooking the quiet little town below.

Jessica surveyed her wardrobe for the seventeenth time that afternoon, and pulled out a sparkly silver top and her favourite jeans. Forget the dress idea – that was not working; she could still look smart in a pair of jeans and her sparkly top. Now, if only she could find that lipstick – it would go perfectly with that top. Oh, and that jacket would go so well with the jeans. The jacket! Of course. Jessica slipped her hand into the jacket pocket. Voila. One pink lipstick. So that was where she had left it. She was fully dressed in a flash and then left pondering which handbag to take. Honestly, the stresses a woman has to face in life – men would never understand.

Another flash of brilliance had Jessica bounding up the stairs to the attic. She had only poked her nose in there briefly last week, but remembered having seen some of Granny's old handbags along with a lot of other old bits and pieces up there. There was a silver clutch purse that had caught her eye, and sure enough, it matched her top beautifully. She took it down to her bedroom and emptied the contents of her own handbag onto the bed. She grabbed her keys, her wallet and her phone, and her lipstick to put in Granny's silver bag. The clasp was a bit stiff to open at first, but after a bit of perseverance and a few choice swear words, the bag opened with a snap. She did not remember Granny ever using this bag and it looked quite old and smelt a little musty. That was nothing a good squirt of perfume would not fix.

She unzipped a little side compartment in the silver purse where she planned to put her lipstick. There was something in there – a bit of paper. No, wait, it was a folded envelope. It must be old, Jessica thought, as the paper had turned yellow with age. She peered closely at the front of it in hope of spotting a postmark date but there was none. In fact the envelope was still sealed, so perhaps it had never been sent. Yes, on closer inspection, the letter was addressed to a Mrs C Turner, and Granny's mother, Ethel Fraser, was the sender. Maybe the clutch purse had been hers? Jessica grabbed her mobile phone to check the time. Hmmm, ten minutes and Gary would be here and she still had not dried her hair. Never mind, her curiosity had got the better of her, and she could not wait another moment to open and read the letter.

She sat on the edge of her bed, and slowly and carefully opened the envelope to reveal a letter, hand-written on pale pink paper in spidery writing which Jessica found difficult to read.

Jessica had seen photos of her great-grandmother but she had died when Jessica was only two so she did not remember her. Granny always spoke fondly of her mother, Ethel.

'Dearest Clara,' the letter read.

'How are you my dear? I trust little Bobby has recovered well from his cold now? Elizabeth misses his friendship terribly. How we all miss you since you moved to the city.

Clara, I have a secret I must share with you as the burden of carrying it alone is too much for me. I dare not tell anyone as I know that will mean the end for Albert. As you know, Elizabeth adores Albert and it would break her heart if she ever found out what he had done, so please don't tell anyone what I am about to share with you.

This terrible news has made me cry for days. The entire ordeal was quite terrifying. Albert has killed dear Georgie. Poor little thing – she was only four. The sad thing is I am sure Albert never meant to hurt her. I don't know quite what happened as Albert has always got on quite well with Georgie, but next thing I knew he had the poor wee thing and was shaking her violently. I don't know what she had done to provoke that sort of behaviour. I shouted at Albert to stop and he looked up and saw me and fled. I ran down the stairs as fast as I could but when I got to Georgie she was already dead.

I panicked. I didn't want anybody to find out, especially Elizabeth, so I got the shovel from the back shed and quickly buried Georgie right there in the back yard next to the oak tree. I know now, that it was a stupid idea and that I would get in a lot of trouble if the truth was ever known. I have been telling everyone that Mr Hampstead had suddenly wanted Georgie back down south and so she had gone back to live with him. Of course I know it to be a huge lie, but how else could I spare Elizabeth's grief at losing Georgie? And if I were to say that Albert killed her, well, then I know that his life would be over for sure. Albert really isn't that bad. He doesn't deserve to be blamed for what happened. At least, I don't think he meant to hurt her. I am sure it must have been a terrible accident.

Oh dear. Clara, what am I to do? Do you think I have done the right thing?

Your true friend Ethel.'

Jessica realised her mouth was hanging open in shock. She could not believe what she had just read. Elizabeth was her grandmother. She had never heard her speak of Georgie or Albert. She wondered who they were. Neighbours or friends, perhaps. She shuddered to think that there was a body buried in the back yard. Whatever had her great grandmother been thinking?

'Gidday Jess. What you got there?' a tall, dark haired man entered the bedroom. Jessica had not heard him come in and she jumped.

'Gary! You scared me half to death. I didn't hear you knock. Sorry.' Jessica showed her boyfriend the letter, explaining how she had come to find it, and who had written it.

'Whoa. This is serious stuff Jess. Do you ever remember your Granny saying anything about a murder here?'

'No,' Jessica replied. 'But I would say she probably never knew about it. In the letter my great-grandmother makes it clear that Granny would be devastated if she ever found out. She must have loved Georgie – and Albert. Oh Gary, do you think the little girl Georgie is still buried outside somewhere? That is too horrible to bare thinking about.'

'Well why don't we go and find out?' Gary suggested.

'Oh don't be so gross! We can't go and dig up a dead body. That is just disgusting.'

'It won't be a body now,' Gary pointed out. 'Just a pile of old bones. Let's go down now and have a poke around. It's quite exciting really. If we find anything we can call the police if you want, but it's not likely that anything can be done about it now. Albert probably died long ago.'

'I'm not going to dig up half of Granny's beautiful garden, looking for something that probably isn't even there. Besides, I wouldn't know where to start looking,' Jessica insisted.

Gary reached over and took the letter from her. Let's start by the oak tree. That's what it says in this letter, right?'

Jessica found herself trudging down the stairs after her boyfriend, protesting loudly about his proposed venture. 'What about the movies? How do I know where to find a spade to use? It's getting dark. What if someone sees us? What if we do find a body – I'm not digging – you can do it! Stupid letter – I wish I'd never told you about it.'

Gary found one of Jessica's Grandmother's spades in the garden shed.

'Is this an oak tree?' Jessica stood at the bottom of the tree, looking up at the gnarled and twisted branches. It was huge and had to be at least 100 years old, she thought. She looked at the house, looming behind the tree. The dusky pink sky framed it with a setting sun, causing shadows to play on the lawn. Windows looked down like eyes, and Jessica wondered where Ethel had been standing when she had looked out from the house to witness the tragedy. Probably one of the bedrooms, she decided. They all faced the back yard and, if Georgie had been killed out the front, any passer-by could have seen from the road.

'Sure is an oak. You can tell by the leaves,' Gary said. 'Now, where should we start digging? Perhaps over closer to the brick wall? Then we can work our way from the wall up to the tree? I don't suppose your great grandmother would have left any marker or headstone for Georgie?'

'Don't be silly,' Jessica replied. 'She didn't want anybody to know Georgie was dead, remember? She tried to hide it from everyone so she would hardly have a huge grave stone!'

'True,' Gary pondered. 'But she obviously cared for little Georgie, so you would think she might have placed something little where she was buried to remember her by. Perhaps the grave site was hidden at the time by a flowering shrub or something.'

Jessica groaned. 'How would we ever know! We are never going to find her. Gary, let's just forget it and go to the movies, please?'

'Not so fast,' Gary was surveying the garden. Behind the magnificent old oak tree was the brick wall that ran around the perimeter of the entire estate. In front of the wall were established shrubs with dense foliage, so as the wall was barely visible. Gary started to rummage under hydrangeas and lift up rhododendron leaves – peering at the ground underneath.

Jessica stood with her hands on her hips, 'What *are* you doing?' She plucked a deep blue petal from her boyfriend's hair before returning her hand to her hip. She was itching to stomp her foot again to gain his attention but decided against it, as her toe still hurt slightly from her earlier stomping that evening. She was wearing her grumpiest face but it was not doing any good because Gary was too busy scratching around at the ground to look at her.

'This is it!' Gary shouted excitedly. 'Look under here, Jess – a small stone slab with something engraved on it. I am trying to brush off the dirt – I am positive that's a 'G'. Come and have a look.'

The light was fading and Jessica wondered if they would need a torch. She knelt down, trying to ignore a feeling of excitement that was pinching at her chest. She felt light headed and realised that she had held her breath and forgotten to breathe. Maybe Gary was not being ridiculous after all – maybe he was on to something. This was scary and exhilarating at the same time. Tiny beads of sweat dotted her forehead as she leant forward and brushed away the dirt and years of dried leaves that had settled on the small concrete slab.

The word appeared slowly as if by magic before their eyes. 'Oh my God, Gary! You're right. It says Georgie. This must be where she is.'

Jessica backed away quickly at the realisation that they had just discovered someone's grave. Before she could protest the shovel bit into the soil. Gary had started digging.

'Don't dig her up,' Jessica pleaded. 'It doesn't seem right somehow. And besides, there is something else engraved in the corner of the concrete slab. It might be a date or something. Let's check that out first.'

'You can check that out. I'll keep digging. I'll be careful, Jess. As soon as I find a bone I'll stop. I don't want to cut the poor wee thing into pieces. Wait – here we go – I think we have found our first bone.' Gary tossed the spade to one side and scrubbed the earth with his fingers to uncover a small thin bone.

'Ok – that's it. You can stop now,' Jessica felt sick.

Gary's fingers were scraped and bleeding but that did not deter his efforts to uncover the truth. 'Hang on for a moment Jess. There is another part here – it is bigger and it might be the skull.'

Jessica's hand went to her mouth. She could not bear to watch anymore so turned her back on her boyfriend and concentrated instead on brushing away the dirt and moss to reveal another engraving on Georgie's tombstone.

'Wait a minute. Something's not quite right here,' Gary sat down on the grass, with part of a small skull in his hand.

'Don't you think that is Georgie?' Jessica asked.

'I think it is Georgie alright, but I think....' Gary took another look at the skull and Jessica realised he was thinking the same thing that she was.

'I think – I don't think this is human.'

'I don't think so either,' Jessica said. 'Have a look at this Gary.' The young man looked at Georgie's tombstone. Jessica had brushed away the dirt to reveal the engraving of a little cat.

'Georgie was a cat!'

Jessica giggled. 'Well, that's kind of a relief. Phew – I thought Georgie was a little girl.'

Gary's eyes darkened. 'Maybe she was, after all.' He had spotted a corner of what looked to be another slab just a little further along from where they had been digging.

'Another grave!' Jessica gasped. Gary scrubbed away to reveal another tombstone, and this one had something lying on it. Jessica wondered if it was an old leather belt or the strap from a handbag. Had it been dumped there, or did it have something to do with Georgie?

Jessica watched as Gary rubbed away under the bushes at the tombstone. Suddenly he sat back laughing.

'What's so funny?' she demanded.

'This one is Alfred's grave,' Gary announced. Then he held up the old leather lead and collar with the name tag still on it. 'And he was a dog!'

NOW AND THEN
Long John Best

I'm guilty, like most, of whinging instead of counting our blessings, that we live at a great time in such a great country as Australia. Hence the following, I've called it, Now and Then. It's an adaptation of a poem I presented at a seminar for the Union of Publique Transport. – **LJB.**

Gee, I'm jack of all those jokers who complain about the drive
From Sydney say to Brisbane, who claim they're tired, when they arrive.
Struth, our roads were never better, motor cars the best they've been.
Spare a thought for those first settlers, when they lobbed on the scene.

The locals all went walkabout, those on water used canoes,
So, they'd not a lot of options, from which they had to choose.
Late in the Eighteenth Century, was when this land first feels
The plodding gait of bullocks and the heavy weight of wheels,

We had no roads prepared for this, for we'd no place to go.
We laid some down round Sydney Town, but us convicts, we'd work slow.
As our population increased, we began to make a push,
To North and South and out we went all heading for the Bush.

The going rough, but folk were tough, back in those early days,
And our dreams relied on bullocks strong; to pull our two-wheeled drays.
Them drivers they could turn a phrase, and I swear that this is true,
'Twas the language used by bullockies, that made our skies so blue.

In the early Eighteen Hundreds, coach lines started to expand.
Now horse drawn, out of village, towns, they moved across this land,
But roadless regions took their toll, springs sprung and axles broke.
Then Freeman Cobb took up the bit, produced his masterstroke.

Imported coaches from the States, slung low on straps of leather,
His big red monsters rode the ruts, day, night, in any weather.
He'd not compete with new laid rail; he'd fill in, in between.
Was his transport integrated? Yes I think it might have been.

Came the middle of the nineteenth, she was on for young and old.
This new colony was struggling, but then we found it. Gold!
Scattered right across this country, in places God forsook,
So we had to go and get it, had to go and have a look.

Needing towns and infrastructure, Diggers needing to be fed,
Needing grog and entertainment, Diggers waiting to be bled,
We used pushbikes, donkeys, camels, anything to ride or pull.
As if a gold rush weren't enough, then came the bloody wool.

Serendipity

We pushed paddle wheelers up to Bourke, no good if in a hurry.
You just might sit the season out, till Darling greets the Murray.
And all the while, the railway lines crept slowly o'er the plains,
And bush folk gathered by the tracks, to cheer the passing trains.

Then omnibus and flatbed trucks appeared on rough bush roads
And Cobb and Co and carriers, watched as they stole their loads.
Off shore stand clippers, rigging slack, their sails now sadly furled,
As steam and motor vessels bear their cargoes round the world.

The Twentieth Century has arrived, and we stand on the brink
Of wars, abroad, not on our shores, the world begins to shrink,
For aviators soar aloft, on wood and fabric wings.
Men, magnifique in their machines, begin to do their things.

Transatlantic, then Pacific, flights of fancy, aircrews die,
Now an everyday occurrence, con trails weave across the sky,
Linking lands of different culture, different colour, different creed,
Intercontinental travel, flown at supersonic speed.

So the next time you go travelling, be it home or overseas,
You remember what you heard to-day, and fellow Aussies please,
Cast your mind back, to those pioneers, who blazed the tracks you take.
Count your blessings, cos compared to theirs, your life's a piece of cake.

FUN IN THE SNOW
Brenda Simcox-Hunt

Jump out of bed to see the snow,
Gleefully running outside,
Fetch our sled, fastest in the street,
Fighting for turns to ride.

Dad made our sled from old bumper bars.
He polished them shiny and bright.
We were so proud, it went so fast,
The others were soon out of sight.

Down in the park, the snowdrifts were deep.
We struggled to the top of the slope.
Ignore freezing hand and frozen feet,
Race down holding tight to the rope.

Steer with our feet to turn left or right,
Snow flies up behind in spray,
Straight into a soft bed of snow.
Oh, what a wonderful day!

Can I have a go? I know what to do.
Her voice was pleading and low.
Press down your right foot to turn to the right
Or into the lake you'll go.

Press down now, to her, we all shriek.
Too late, she didn't obey.
Straight into the lake where the ice was weak.
Wet feet. That was the end of her day.

VERTICAL BLUE

Belinda Janz

THE day started like any other on this holiday. Breakfast had been delivered late to our room, without the newspaper; at least the coffee made the wait bearable. We decided last night that if our breakfast was delayed again then we were going to check out and try another place up the road. After all, you do not come to the Bahamas for this.

As I stared out across to the distant ocean view of our supposed waterfront room, it occurred to me that we had not received our complimentary champagne and fresh fruit on arrival, and it was day four already. We had enjoyed peace and rest as the place was quiet. Yesterday only three other people had joined us for the *Learn to Dive Experience* in the pool.

My husband and I had completed a weekend beginner's diving course years before our business in land management moved to the southern part of Chocolate Mountain. Working in the desert gave us no chance to further our skills. We felt a beginner's course may be what we needed before following up on recommended dive sites around the island. We were to have another dive lesson that day but I was keen to explore other accommodation.

My husband said he would follow up on the Vertical Blue diving course to see if they had any beginner classes starting soon, while I looked for other accommodation.

My walk took me along a little winding path behind one of the pink sand beaches. Against the back drop of the splendid blues in the ocean, I soon drifted off in dreamy thoughts. I wandered along a trail that slowly led me up onto higher ground and away from the township. We had been told about some grottos or hot tubs out this way. I decided to see if I could find them. I enjoyed the adventure of discovering new places and, after being in the desert for so long, I think we both felt we needed a sea-change holiday to refresh our batteries after a long hot summer.

In no time at all I came across the rocky pools of water. We were told that the pools filled up at high tide, so that when the tide goes back out, some water is left trapped in the rugged landscape of holes – big enough to be used as natural hot tubs.

I looked around and, seeing no one else, decided to take off my dress and slip into the nearest pool. I had not considered wearing swimmers when I had decided on the walk but thought I could get away with black underwear, even if someone did happen to come along. The water was a lot hotter than I expected and quite relaxing for my muscles. I could see boats in the distance bobbing along like little ducks in a big blue bath, as I looked out to the Atlantic from the cliff edge.

I stretched out and tried to lie back against the edge of the pool but found the rock unwelcoming. As I sat up to readjust, I noticed a gust of wind had caught my dress and was blowing it across the rocks towards the cliff edge. In a panic, I jumped up out of the pool, scraping my knee. I went after the dress. Without thinking about my movements, I reached over to save the dress now at the cliff edge, and that was when everything went blank.

When I came around, I was stretched out on a hard base. A man seemed to be talking to me and I saw him hold up my arm. Even though I was sure it was my arm, I felt nothing. There was no sound attached to his moving lips. I must have passed out again, though I have no idea for how long.

The next time I woke up I appeared to be in a hospital room with several people. My husband I recognized but the other men were strangers. This time, I could hear their voices talking in low whispers. I went to talk but my voice seemed stuck in my throat and could only manage a bit of a cough. My husband rushed straight over. He started stroking my face and kissing my forehead, obviously relieved at my consciousness.

I closed my eyes and slipped back into a more relaxed state. After a while I opened my eyes to see the strangers had gone from the room but another man had entered.

He introduced himself as a doctor. He explained that I had had a fall. I was lucky I had fallen clear of the rocky cliff edge and even luckier to be found by a diving class in the area. With that I fell asleep again and only woke up many hours later, feeling decidedly hungry.

My husband called the doctor on duty in to see me. This doctor explained that, while it was a good sign that I felt hungry, I was not allowed to eat. They wanted to run some more tests to follow up on something that had showed up in a scan. The doctor said that I had mentioned to one of the divers who had rescued me that I had been up at the top of the cliff in a hot pool before feeling faint and as a result somehow fell over the cliff edge.

I remembered trying to stop my dress from blowing over the edge, and then, as I had gone down to grab at it, had just passed out.

Luckily I was in a relaxed state, the doctor said. He suggested that, when I had got out of the hot water into the cold wind, I may have experienced a disruption in the balance of neurotransmitters that regulate the blood vessels and heart rate, causing a temporary decrease in blood flow to the brain. This could have caused me to faint. It sounded unusual to me. The doctor said that they just wanted to run some more tests to make sure it was nothing more sinister.

By the following afternoon, with more rest and tests, I was in a better place to understand what had happened. When I had passed out and fallen, I had been lucky that the part of the cliff jutted out over its base below and I had fallen clean into the water in a relaxed state. A man, a member of a diving class on a boat, saw me. The group was part of an Intermediate Free Diving Course from the Vertical Blue School, the very school my husband had been going to see that same day. The school did not often come to this island for classes but had decided to take the students across to the secluded area that day for a practical session of yoga and relaxation underwater. The men in my hospital room the first day I had woken were from the Vertical Blue School team.

The test results came back marked for urgent attention. It seems one of the Vertical Blue trainer's brother was a doctor at this hospital. How lucky I was, the doctor said. The tests showed that I had an abnormal heart muscle valve, something that could easily be fixed with surgery. The doctor suspected that I was born with the faulty valve, not as uncommon as you may think. The lucky thing was that it had been discovered now, as a deep dive may have put a lot more pressure on the valve. If I had passed out underwater while diving, things could have turned out very differently.

So was the doctor suggesting how serendipitous it was for me that we had been dissatisfied with our accommodation that I had gone off in search of alternatives, before getting into a hot pool which would ultimately end in me falling off a cliff while chasing my dress?

I smiled to myself, and admitted yes, I had been lucky. I had been rescued almost straight away and given good hospital care which discovered the cause of my blackout. To add to the whole lucky thing, the owner of our accommodation heard about our story and was able to explain why the breakfasts were late each day. They were respecting our privacy, knowing from previous experience most guests like to sleep in late and enjoy a simpler meal. As for the champagne and fresh fruit, it was an oversight. A change-over in staff occurred when the lady who normally looked after our room went on maternity leave. To show how hospitable the people were, the owner offered us not only an extra free day stay but lent his car to my husband to use when I was coming out of the hospital. He himself drove us to the airport when we left.

My surgery was straight forward, as the doctor had said. Almost six months later, having fully recovered and returned to work, I smiled in reflection of our plan to get away on a relaxing holiday and get back into diving.

It would not be long before it was holiday time again; I wondered what relaxing underwater yoga was like.

DON'T SPEAK TO THE HAND
Lorraine Noscov

'OH pll-eease Jennifer. Stop!' Marion stated firmly. Jennifer ignored her and continued talking about her latest failed relationship. After listening and nodding and shaking her head for another twenty minutes, Marion sprung out of her chair and held her hand in front of Jennifer's face. Even this action did not stop Jennifer talking as she tried to push Marion's hand away. She then stopped talking about "woe is me" stuff and grabbed Marion's hand and asked, 'What's with this?'

Silence reigned for a couple of seconds then Jennifer shook Marion's hand and in an aggrieved tone, repeated 'What's with this? So rude! You have such nerve! How dare you hold your hand in front of my face while I am talking to you? I thought you were my best friend. Here I am confiding in you all about my deepest personal hurtful feelings and what do you do? You hold your hand in front of my face. I really value your opinions and your advice and now, when I really have to figure a way to get back with Neil, you do this. I really need your advice. I have no-one to...'

Marion moved her hand away quickly and her face appeared in its place.

Jennifer gasped.

Marion said, 'Jennifer, stop! You have talked non-stop since you got here over an hour ago. If you really want my advice, then stop talking long enough for me to be able to say something.'

Jennifer went to speak. Marion placed her hand back in front of her face. Once again Jennifer gasped.

Marion continued. 'For years, you have come to me with all your woes. I have sat quietly and listened, made a thousand cups of coffee for you in that time, and often when you have been here for a long visit, I have fed you. Other times you have phoned me and I have listened to you for hours.'

Jennifer angrily tried to shake Marion's hand and said, 'I have appreciated all those times and your friendship. Marion, please move your hand and please don't replace it with your face again. You stunned me when you did that. I have never had someone stand so close to me and speak to me the way you have just done. You really were and are being quite rude. Yes, I do want your advice but you could wait till I stop talking. I really did not have much more to say. Marion, please move your hand. It is very difficult to talk about my feelings and how I plan to get Neil back with your hand being so close to my face.'

Marion interrupted and once again said firmly, 'Oh pll-eease, Jennifer. Stop! Enough is enough. Right now the best advice I can give for us both is to get you to shush. Don't talk. Don't say anything.'

'Oh Marion, what has got into you? You are so rude today. I am so broken-hearted. Neil meant the world to me. I did everything for him. Most of all I never let him feel alone in this harsh world. I know what that feels like and I hate the thought of those I hold dear having to cope with...'

This time Marion's voice exploded in a deep heavy-volumed sound as she ordered, 'Stop! Shut up! Just shut your mouth!'

Jennifer sat back in her chair, her mouth trying to form a word which Marion saw and quickly and harshly repeated, 'Stop!' Again she saw Jennifer's mouth twitching to open and she scowled and shook her head and growled, 'No, no!'

Silence.

Once again Jennifer's mouth twitched and again Marion growled, 'No, no!'

One minute of absolute silence after hours of listening to someone feeling sorry for themselves and their scheming and conniving plans is like having a holiday away from all pain and pressure.

Relief.

Marion inhaled deeply. Jennifer shifted in her chair and received a glare from Marion who then spoke. 'Enough is enough. As I said before, I have listened to you for years, but now, no more. I cannot do this anymore. Last month, I was going through an extremely hurtful time and I phoned you. All you said to me was that I called you at a very inconvenient time and you did not have the time to talk.'

Jennifer tried to speak but Marion put her hand up again and continued. 'This was not the first time. In fact, most times I have called you, it has been inconvenient for you and yet when you phone me or just visit on the spur of the moment, I have to drop everything and listen to you.

'Years ago, I used to text you, but I stopped this also and have only replied to your texts. It did not take me long to realise that when I sent you a text to say "hi" or to say "how are you" you never replied. Yet when you needed to text me, a few times I did not reply to your messages immediately and I remember you got so mad at me. Each time you ended up calling me and telling me that I was being ignorant by not replying instantly. When we first met, you often just visited me when you felt like it. Oh, you still do this.

'Way back then, I visited you a couple of times without calling first and you were not happy about me just "popping in". For the last few years, I have not called you unless you have requested me to do so. I have not "popped in" to visit. The only text messages I have sent to you have been in reply to ones you have sent to me.

'Well last week was the final straw. I really needed to talk, but, after my brush off from you, I went to The Blue Diamond Café to have a quiet cup of tea. Funny how Fate plays out. If you had listened to me, I would still be living my same old life. Through circumstances at that café, my life now has new opportunities. I won't bother to tell you about them, as today – and every day – is all about you.

'My advice to you is to just plain stop all your feeling sorry for yourself. Stop all your conniving and scheming plans to get Neil back. From what I know now, if you and he are meant to be together, somehow the Universe seems to shuffle things around and you both will find yourselves in the same unusual situation at the same time and you both will know that something greater than yourselves is at work.'

'Oh Marion, I do believe that something happened to you at the café and whatever it was has certainly had a great effect on you. You are now rude, short-tempered and now it seems as if you believe in fantasy. Believing in Fate, destiny or whatever it is called, is silly. Next you will start talking about Angels, spirits, ghosts and fortune telling. You know how I feel about all this stuff. I believe you have to work out your own problems and if that means, as you said, conniving and scheming ways to make things happen then this is what I do. I do not believe in sitting and waiting for things to happen.'

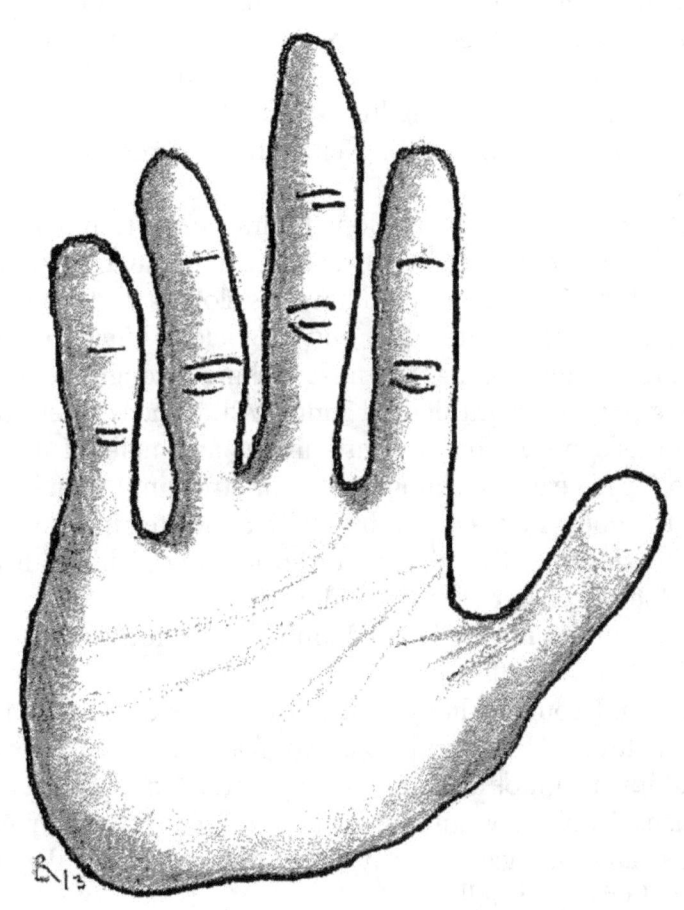

Marion raised her hand. This time Jennifer blocked the hand with her arm and continued talking.

'As for you saying you never call me to talk, well that is totally untrue. You have always called me at Christmas and my birthdays and when I have been sick. I have always been polite to you. I don't remember the last time you called. If I said it was an inconvenient time then it must have been. I am not a liar. You know that when I am in a relationship I put all of my energies into it. Why, I even stop having long lunches with friends as you well know. Keeping my man and keeping him satisfied and happy are the most important things to me. With Neil, I tried harder than with any other man.

'As you know, he works long hours. Gone from home by 7am and since his promotion he does not get home till 8pm, totally exhausted. I made sure he would have his clothes for the next day all laid out ready in the spare room and a delicious lunch in the fridge. He loved my home cooking. I so miss looking through recipes to find something new he might like for lunch. Ah! Sundays were the best. He would ask me to cook a roast dinner and make a dessert. He would go for his early morning five-kilometre run. When he came in through the door, I always met him with an ice tea in summer and a hot tea in winter. I did this as I loved looking at him, all hot and sweaty'. She closed her eyes and sighed.

Marion did not hesitate. 'Jennifer, I do not want to hear any more. For the years I have known you, yes, I have rung you for Christmas and your birthdays but not once have you ever rung me for my birthday. I know all your woes about each of your failed relationships. I cannot listen to you anymore. Jennifer, I need you to go, please. Don't say anything, just leave.' Marion picked up Jennifer's handbag, gave it to her and pointed to the door saying, 'Goodbye, I wish you well.'

Jennifer was stunned but left quietly.

Marion walked into her lounge room, picked up a photo and recalled the day at the café when she was feeling slightly depressed.

This man walked up to her and said, 'You are beautiful. May I take your photo?' She had agreed as long as she would be able to have a copy. He gave her his business card after he wrote his personal number on the back of it. They had met again a few days later. He told her that the day he saw her it had been a strange day.

Each move he had made, he felt he had made before. Then when he entered the café, just to buy a cold drink and leave, he saw her.

If Jennifer had listened to Marion for even five minutes, she would never have met this man who seemed mesmerised by her. That was three months ago.

Today, he had phoned earlier to say he wanted to see her that evening as he had something very important to ask her. All she could think to herself was that to meet this man, she was in the right place at the right time. Thanks to Jennifer.

BLOODY TINNY BUGGER
Carole Young

THE bar of the local RSL had only three customers on Monday morning. It was air-conditioned but I could still smell the residue of years of beer spillages under the cloying air freshener. My photographer and I had been sent to get a human interest piece a week out from Anzac Day. That's right – I, Lisa Hume, am a reporter for the local paper. The editor, Bill Mitchell, thought the RSL was the most likely place to find a story relating to war.

Last year, my human interest story held up the front page. But it turned out that the fellow I interviewed had made up the story of an uncle missing in action because he thought that was what we wanted. It was a shame the story appeared on the front page. My humiliation began with the first phone call stating that Wally Newman, the supposed missing uncle, had never gone to war and had lived all his life in the district. The locals thought it was strange that my source, his nephew, did not know that.

So there we were, Mike Parker and I, in the bar of the RSL surveying three likely candidates for a story. All three were nursing pots of beer at the bar. It was just on 10.30am but they looked very comfortable on their stools. We approached the fellow who sat the farthest away.

I introduced Mike and myself and waited for the man to acknowledge us. The old man just sat on his stool with both hands around his glass. His hat lay on the stool beside him. He looked in his eighties, his skin was covered in liver spots and wrinkles. He wore no glasses. Little sprouts of hair, the same gunmetal grey as the sparse hair on his head, came from his nose and ears.

I broke the silence and jumped right in. 'Can I ask you a few questions about the war?' The man ignored us. The barman moved down the bar and motioned us away.

'He's missing his mate,' the barman said. 'I don't think you'll get anything out of him.'

I turned back to the old man. He was just the fellow I was looking for. Mateship! Sacrifice! My buttons were going off! How do I get to his?

I waved the barman off with what I hoped was an understanding look and went back to the old man. I put my hand on his shoulder and tried again to engage him. 'I'm sorry about your loss. Can you tell me about your friend?'

The old man shook his head and without turning to me said, 'Never knew another bloke like him. Bloody tinny bugger!'

I waited for more but none came as the old man stared into his empty glass. Mike understood. 'What are you drinking old digger?'

The old man looked at Mike and he smiled, revealing a yellow picket fence. His eyes were watery but alight as he said, 'Bundy rum with a beer chaser.'

Mike signalled the barman who had overheard. We waited until the barman had put the drinks in front of the old man. I was just about to launch my first question when the old man turned to Mike, saluted him with the tot glass and said, 'Thanks young fella.' He downed the rum in one gulp. His gnarly hands went straight to caress the pot of beer. He lifted the glass in salute and said, 'Here's to Snow!' He drank thirstily.

I thought, *he'll be drunk before I can get anything out of him.*

Mike sensed my unease and said, 'Lisa would like to hear about your mate'.

The old man screwed his eyes up and looked at me. 'You wouldn't understand, Girly,' he said and took a sip of his beer.

'My Dad is a Vietnam vet,' I lied. The old man put his glass down and licked his lips.

'What unit?' He looked me in the eye.

I don't know about anything military but I knew I had to convince him. 'Light Horse,' I said, thinking of those feathers on the hats on Anzac Day.

'Three Cav!' Mike jumped in. 'Armoured personnel carriers.' I blinked Mike a silent thank-you. The old man eyed me warily, but he appeared to trust Mike. 'What do you want to know?' he said to me, while nodding at Mike.

'What was your friend's name, and how did you meet?' I took out my notebook and pencil and switched my recorder on. The old man – we learned his name was Bill Long – began his story about his mate Alf "Snow" Short. Yes, the best mates copped their share of jokes because of their names.

'Me and Snow first met at Sydney Showgrounds in November 1940 when we were both mustered into the 2/12th Field Ambulance – the "body snatchers" they called us. A field ambulance is the spear point of the army medical system. Although we didn't carry arms we could find ourselves in the front line during a big enemy advance or a withdrawal. Our mob was formed from militia light horsemen from the bush. We wore the plumes in our hats like your Dad.'

He looked at me to see if I appreciated that he, like my Dad, had once been a mounted soldier before he continued.

'Snow was tall and wiry and I was short and stumpy. Snow had a head of curly blond hair and his eyes were Reckitts' Blue. When he laughed everyone laughed with him. You couldn't help it.' (Mike later told me Reckitt & Sons made washing blue in Australia from the 19th century.)

Bill guffawed himself into a snort at the memory. 'We both came from the bush, good with our hands and as inventive as men of the bush need to be. I worked for my old man on a little sheep run but Snow worked for a cow cocky. I think he wanted to be his own boss.'

The old man continued his story and we learned that Snow was the tinniest bloke Bill had ever known. He could lose a bob and find a quid! (Australian currency roughly equivalent to 10 cents and two dollars, Mike told me later) But Bill said Snow was a good bloke, who never said a bad word about anyone if he could not say a good one. And he could handle himself in a fight. Bill could not beat a carpet so it was prudent for him to stick to Snow. And Snow could pull the girls. He did not say a lot but he looked like he knew plenty.

On Boxing Day in 1940 the unit was sent to Cowra, NSW, for training, before heading to the Northern Territory in March 1941. The troops travelled by train through Victoria to Terowie in South Australia where they spent a few days before travelling to Alice Springs by train. The trip by road to Darwin was long, arduous and perilous with washouts.

The unit was attached to 23rd Infantry Brigade of the 8th Division and they should have gone to Malaya to join the rest of the Division but were held back in Australia. Only two brigades were sent to Malaya and the third brigade of the 8th Division stayed in the

Northern Territory with its support units until Japan entered the war.

The men camped at Winellie in Darwin. With no medical work to do, they were employed alongside engineers and infantry assault pioneers in building roads and infrastructure for the troops fortifying and staging through the Northern Territory. It was not long before morale was as low among the 2/12th as it was among the troops already there. Gambling and drinking were popular pastimes to ease the boredom.

Snow used to play two-up and poker and he was just about unbeatable. Only thing was he never seemed to have any money. So Bill staked him and the pals split the winnings. Snow had a Midas touch. Bill could not understand why Snow never seemed to have any money. It took Bill a while to realise that when the winnings were split the stake was included so Bill only got half his stake money back, sometimes even less.

The simultaneous Japanese attacks on Pearl Harbour and Malaya changed the outlook and focus on Australia's northern defences. The three infantry battalions of the 23rd Brigade were sent to Rabaul, (2/22nd) which is on New Britain in the Solomon Islands, and the islands of Ambon (2/21st) and Timor (2/40th) to Australia's north-west.

The engineers and field ambulance men attached to the 23rd Brigade were sent in support. Forty five men of 2/12th were sent to Ambon and the same number went to Timor, reducing the unit to half its strength.

It was not long before Ambon and Rabaul fell to the Japanese armies and the troops were either killed or captured. An attempt was made to reinforce the garrison at Timor but the convoy of troop ships was attacked by aircraft and turned back for Darwin. Bill and Snow laboured on, unscathed on the outside, each silently thanking the Fates for their good fortune.

The old man stopped his narration and looked knowingly at his empty beer glass. I looked at Mike. He gave me a look that said "You owe me" and said, 'Same again Bill?' to which the yellow picket fence appeared again.

The drink ritual was repeated and Snow was toasted before old Bill took up his story again.

After Rabaul, Ambon, Malaya and Singapore fell, all of the men felt the loss of their pals. But the news of the rapid Japanese advance on a wide front and the frantic activity in camp and on infrastructure left little time for the troops to grieve. They also made the most of their down time lest they too end up "in the bag" as they referred to capture.

The Japanese bombed Darwin four days after Singapore fell. The troops had not recovered from the shock of the first attack when the Japs launched another.

The men of 2/12th were kept busy sorting dead from wounded and then putting their skills to use. An exodus of non-combatants and some military personnel streamed south. When news finally started to filter in to Darwin the mates learned that Timor had fallen.

Military installations in the Northern Territory mushroomed as the territory was flooded with troops to repel a Japanese invasion. An all-weather road was built from Alice Springs to Darwin. The bombing continued and spread to north Queensland and the north of Western Australia. The military machine played catch-up with the Japanese.

Civilian women had been evacuated after the bombing so only service women were left. There were slim pickings as the nurses were officers and there were few women the enlisted boys could pursue. Flies and endless boredom were their usual companions.

When their tour of the Territory came to an end, the 2/12th Field Ambulance was sent to Reid Town, north of Wollongong in NSW early in 1943. The trip back by road to Alice Springs was made on the new all-weather highway. The boys were pleasantly surprised. They entrained at Alice Springs for Sydney via Terowie, South Australia. Troop movement control was well co-ordinated by this time and the boys were well fed and "watered" all the way back to Sydney.

When on leave from the Reid Town camp, the troops could swim without the fear of crocodiles and did not have to lob a grenade into the water to clear it of them. They didn't have to duck any bombs, either. But the opportunities to spend money were many and varied now and the amenities available obviated the need to gamble among themselves to ease the boredom. Bill and Snow's funds gained through gambling dried up somewhat. Bill figured that

Snow had amassed over 800 quid but he still seemed to have nothing to show for it. At least nothing that was evident to Bill. Any attempts Bill made to find out what Snow did with his money bore no fruit.

On a brilliant sunny day, Bill and Snow were on a beach north of the "Gong" when Snow lazily picked up a large helmet shell of a sea snail. He rolled it in his fingers admiring the dark brown bands on the glossy light tan background. He shook the shell and took a closer look at it then slid it into his pocket.

Later, back at camp Bill ambled after Snow when he went over to the ambulance drivers' workshop and asked if he could use the vice. Bill was surprised when Snow took the shell from his pocket, put it into the jaws of the vice and slowly applied pressure enough to crack it in half. Bill's mouth dropped open when Snow picked a ring out of the broken pieces of shell. He held it up to the light and said, 'That will come in handy!' Bill thought it was an engagement ring. It had a big square stone in a big silver band. The tinny bloody bugger!

The ring was soon forgotten when the troops received a "movement warning" and got brief pre-embarkation leave. Furphies, as rumours were called, were winging through the camp as the boys packed for their leave. Five ships had already been sunk off their part of the coast by enemy action since the beginning of the year and more had been sunk further up the coast. The odds were good that they were going to New Guinea. That move had to be made by ship.

The unit was at full strength again, complete with its Service Corps section of ambulance drivers. The officer scheduling the transfer of stores and equipment ordered that the ambulances be returned to the motor pool as they would not accompany the troops. Furphies flew over the *latrine wireless* that there were no roads where they were going. The most credible bit of info came from the quartermaster's office. Bill had opined that it was dangerous to travel by ship up the coast and the orderly had said, 'Not this time, mate. We're on the new Hospital Ship! She'll be lit up like a King's Cross brothel so there will be no mistakes!'

Snow reminded Bill that the Hospital Ship *Manunda* had been bombed in Darwin and the 119th General Hospital had been strafed, despite the huge red cross on the roof. *Manunda* had been near legitimate targets but there was no mistaking the hospital for what it was. The men wanted to believe that "mistakes" would not occur to their hospital ship alone at sea.

As the men paraded before entraining for the dock at Darling Harbour, Corporal Short and Pte Long were "told off" to fall out for special duty. They learned that they were to travel to Townsville by train to embark with additional stores when the ship pulled in to her only Australian port of call before she went on to New Guinea.

The main body of the unit embarked on the Australian Hospital Ship *Centaur* on 10 May 1943 while the mates were at Central Station in Sydney handing over their orders to the Railway Transport Officer. The pals had to cool their heels for two days before they got transport as far as South Brisbane where they had to report to the RTO for entraining for Townsville. In Brisbane the RTO told the pair that their orders had been changed to meet the ship in Cairns.

Bill stopped his narration and took a sip of his beer. This one had lasted longer than the previous, thank Heaven. His memory of events so long ago was crystal clear and his recounting was easy to listen to and follow. I liked the old man's self-deprecating honesty. He got straight back to his story.

'When we got to South Brisbane we saw all these black Yanks. The blokes at the pub told us the black Yanks weren't allowed to go over the river. There had been a big blue between the Yanks and the Aussies. The Yanks had a stranglehold on the girls.

Thanks to Snow we took a couple of girls to the pictures and had a good time until the train left for Cairns. It was a long and slow trip up north. The train was often shunted while supply and ambulance trains went through. We got to Townsville on 19th May and had a few at the railway pub. A bloke came in and told us that the Prime Minister had told Parliament that the Japs sank the *Centaur*!'

I was shocked by the look on Bill's face but Mike looked as if he was expecting this news. As I said, I know nothing about things military but I was shocked myself that a Hospital Ship would be attacked. Bill teared up. He wiped his eyes before he continued.

'All our mates! All those nurses! Bastards! We didn't carry weapons in the FA but if I had seen a Jap when we heard the news I'd have killed him with my bare hands. The ship was torpedoed on 14 May off Cape Moreton. The Yanks picked up some survivors after a day and a half. There weren't many. Only one nurse! It took a while before the number of casualties became clear. Wrong numbers were quoted for a long time. Me and Snow were included in the numbers with 18 other blokes who were not on board. There were 332 souls on board and only 64 saved. Only 14 of the 179 men of the unit were picked up. The Red Cross had meant nothing!'

Bill picked up his glass and drained it. He sat with his head down. None of us spoke. This time I respected the silence. After a while, I asked Bill if he would like some lunch. He nodded and we found a table in the dining room. While we waited for our lunch Mike bought some drinks, only a beer this time for Bill. I took up my glass of squash and asked, 'What happened to you boys after that?'

'Things just weren't the same after that. The unit got rebuilt again but we stayed in Australia until we went to Borneo in 1945. It was hard for the new blokes at first. They just weren't the old blokes. Having lost mates twice, we were a bit leery about making more mates. It wasn't their fault but we couldn't help it, ya know?

'Borneo was a piece of cake for us until we got to Kuching and learned about our mates who were captured. Lucky the Japs never came within cooee of me. Snow too. Some of the new blokes were given the job if we had to deal with the Japs but we were soon sent back to Morotai. We helped to repatriate the prisoners until we came home.

'Me and Snow went back to the bush. I found out what he'd done with his money. He saved it and bought a spread of his own. He got married to a nurse he met on Morotai. I married a war widow from me 'ome town. We both moved to the Big Smoke when the bush went sour after the Government shut down the railway.'

Our lunch arrived and we tucked in. We were spending a lot of time on this interview, our expenses were starting to add up, as well. We ate in silence while I tried a layout of the story in my head. I decided the pathos level was perfect but would build it up. It would focus on the *Centaur* even though Bill and Snow had not been on the ship. Bill paired his cutlery and used his napkin before I spoke.

'What happened to Snow?' I asked as gently as I could.

'His Missus died.'

'When was this, didn't he take it very well?' I could imagine the man to be grief stricken.

'Six months back. Oh! He took it well enough!' Bill clenched his jaw as if in pain. 'It was the bloody ring. He gave it to his wife when they got engaged. He had to have everything valued for her Estate. Turns out the ring was worth a coupla million. It was some old, ancient thing.'

Stunned I said 'Weren't you happy for him?'

'Course I was. But he sold it and bought a flamin' pub for his son to run on the Gold Coast! That's where he is now, the bloody tinny bugger!'

_____ooo_____

ON our way back to the car I asked Mike what "tinny" meant.

He looked at me with surprise as though I should have known before he said, 'Lucky – Very lucky! Haven't you heard about a person being so tinny they'd rust if they came in contact with water?' he laughed.

I thought about the boys and the fate that they had avoided and said, 'They weren't lucky. They were blessed!'

'What about Snow's ring? That was a heap of luck.'

'No,' I said. 'That was serendipity. I'd say he was **very** blessed!'

MY LOVE

Brenda Simcox-Hunt

I HAD one last luxurious stretch in the warm perfumed bath, stood up and brushed off the excess water. I wrapped myself in a soft fluffy bath robe and walked into the bedroom. My Love came and gave me a quick kiss and a hug saying, 'I have poured your wine; it's on the patio. Have a look at the sunset; it's magic.'

I walked onto the patio and sat on the swing, sipping my wine. I gazed at the sun setting over the sea, thinking what a heavenly place this is for a honeymoon. Without realizing it, my mind drifted back to my first marriage and the lovely honeymoon we had had then.

Adam and I were blissfully happy and had a very romantic honeymoon. We thought our love would last forever.

I do not remember when things first began to go wrong; we were both so busy with our careers and having a good time. Both being teachers, we had so much in common from the start. We liked the same music, read the same kind of books and loved the same kind of food. We both enjoyed cooking too. It was natural for us to fall in love.

We were married within a year of our meeting. The first two years were bliss. We did everything together with our crazy friends, and we had such fun. Our parents kept dropping hints about babies but we were content with each other and did not want babies yet.

Then little things began to niggle at us. I would get fed up with Adam not putting the toilet seat down. He hated me hanging my undies in the shower at night. I got angry every time he did the washing and refused to put conditioner in the last rinse. He said he did not like us using too many chemicals.

Then *she* started at his school. He would say Donna this and Donna said that until I got sick of hearing her name. I got so mad one day I threw the book I was reading at his head. He got up and walked out of the house.

He did not come home that night. I imagined all sorts of things, thinking he had gone to Donna's or he had had an accident. He came in about 7.30 next morning.

'Where were you last night?' I asked him.

'I stayed over at Matt's place,' he answered. He went into the shower and I followed him in accusing him of all sorts of things. He would not talk to me while he got dressed as I continued to rant and rave at him. I realized afterwards that I had said some terrible things to him, accusing him of having an affair with Donna.

'If that is what you think, there is no point in me trying to discuss this with you anymore.' He threw a few clothes in a suitcase and walked out.

I did try to talk to him a few times afterwards but he said he was so hurt by my saying he had had an affair that he could not see any future for us together. Then, of course, me and my big mouth, I said I would divorce him, hoping that would make him talk to me.

He proved he was just as stubborn and pig headed as I was. 'Don't bother, I will divorce you instead,' he calmly told me.

Our friends tried their best to get us together again but I was terribly hurt that he did not even try to reason with me. Neither of us would cooperate with any of their plans for reconciliation and we were divorced just fifteen months later.

I still saw a lot of our friends and they told me Adam lived a very quiet life. He did not go out much other than going to dinner at our friends' homes. Some of them said I had made a big mistake by not pursuing him but I said evidently he did not want me as he had not tried to pursue me.

Then I met Hal, big cuddly comfortable Hal. He was so different to Adam. Nothing worried him. He was happy to do whatever I wanted to do. We never argued. He was never late, always brought me flowers and treated me like a princess. I felt so protected and safe with Hal. When we had been going out together for a year he asked me to marry him. I said yes. My friends tried to tell me I was making a big mistake but I would not listen to them. How could I be making a mistake, when Hal loved me and was willing to do anything for me? But, to satisfy them and my parents, I agreed to a six months' engagement.

One weekend, when Hal was staying over at my flat, I asked, 'What do you want to do tonight?'

He replied, 'I am happy to do whatever you want to do.'

I felt a trickle of fear. Was this what my life with Hal was going to be like? With me making all the decisions and Hal always giving in to me? Adam and I used to have some good arguments but it was always fun making up again and he liked me to be independent of him. I began to wonder if I was doing the right thing by marrying Hal. I thought my life would be boring with him and I did not think I could cope with that.

It was three months before our wedding and Hal wanted to begin to make plans. He wanted us to have a marriage-celebrant service in Chloe and Jim's beautiful garden at Samford. Jim was Hal's older brother. He is just like Hal. Jim and Chloe lived a very ordinary life on acreage. Jim worked from home and Chloe stayed home to mind their six kids. They were so happy with each other. They were a beautiful family and I liked them a lot but I knew that kind of life was not for me. I asked Hal for more time before we made any plans.

New Year's Eve was coming up. Steve and Jan organized a big masquerade party. Hal and I were invited. Hal wanted to go to a family do at Jim's house but I really wanted to do something outrageous for a change. Hal agreed to go with me. Then two days before the party, there was a huge cyclone up north and Hal was asked to go up to help. He is an electrician for an electricity supplier. I was sad to see him go but he is such a caring man I knew he wanted to go to help in any way he could.

My girlfriends asked me to go to the party with them. Hal said I should go. I was very excited but I did feel guilty going without him.

Everyone had made a big effort with their costumes; it was hard to tell who was who. I had a wonderful time. I really let my hair down for the first time since my divorce.

On the stroke of midnight I was in the middle of the crowd and everyone was kissing one another. I didn't even think about Hal. A man in a Phantom costume came over, grabbed me, held me tightly and kissed me. As soon as he kissed me I knew it was Adam. He kissed me with such loving tenderness I realized that I still loved him and the way he was kissing me, he still loved me, too. We just held onto each other and kissed and kissed even when the music died down. Our friends gave a cheer and clapped their hands. The rest of the night passed in a lovely blur. Adam asked if he could take me home. As much as I would have loved him to, I said no in respect for Hal.

We met for lunch the next day and talked about how we were going to tell Hal that I had changed my mind. I felt dreadful. I knew Hal loved me dearly and I was very fond of him.

'You'll have to tell him as soon as he comes home,' Adam said to me.

'I know I will, but it will be very hard. I am very fond of him.'

'Are you sure you want to break off your engagement? I'll understand if you don't want to.'

I felt scared. 'Don't you want us to get back together again?' I asked in a trembling voice.

Adam grabbed both my hands in his. 'Of course I do. I have thought of nothing else since we divorced. When I heard you were engaged, I thought my heart would break into little pieces. When Steve told me about the New Year's Eve fancy dress party, I knew it was my chance to try to make you see how much I loved you.'

I squeezed his hands tight. 'My darling, I didn't realize how much I loved you until you kissed me.'

We had not finished our lunch but Steve said, 'Let's get out of here.'

He put fifty dollars on the table and we walked out. The sun was shining on the sea over the road. We walked over and sat on a bench. He held me to his chest. 'How do you want to tell Hal?'

'I want to tell him face to face. He will phone me tonight, so I don't know how I will get out of telling him then.'

'If he asks, tell him you had a lovely time at the party and try to change the subject.'

'I will but I won't be able to lie to him.'

Holding each other close, we sat and watched the sea flowing onto the shore. It was wonderful but it was also very sad as I knew I had to tell Hal that I had changed my mind. Late in the afternoon Adam drove me home. He did not ask me if I wanted him to come in.

'When will Hal be home? Do you know yet?'

'That's what he will tell me tonight. I think they may all fly home tomorrow.'

'Do you want to go out to dinner tonight? Or would you rather be alone?'

'I think I would rather be alone. I need to think how I will tell him.'

'I understand, my darling. Will I call you after 10 tonight?'

'Yes that would be lovely. I will probably need cheering up by then.'

I kissed him briefly and ran inside. My stomach was churning and I was feeling sick.

I was so nervous I could not eat any dinner. Pouring myself a glass of wine, I sat on the lounge and pretended to watch TV. The phone rang just after eight. My hands were shaking as I switched on my mobile. 'Hello.' I felt breathless

'How's my beautiful girl? It's so good to hear your voice.'

'Hello Hal. It's good to hear from you too. How did everything go? When are you coming home?'

'We will be flying into Brisbane on the 10am flight tomorrow. Will you be able to get time off work to pick me up, Sweetheart?'

'Yes, I'll be there. Was it awful? Was there a lot of damage?'

'It wasn't as bad as I thought it would be. I've got to go now; all the boys are going out to dinner, so I'll see you tomorrow then?'

'Yes, see you at 10 in the morning. Goodbye, Dear.'

'Dear? Is that the best you can do?'

'I'm sorry. I'm not feeling very well at the moment. Think I had too much wine last night.'

'Okay, Sweetheart. Have an early night and I'll see you tomorrow.'

'Bye,' I mumbled but he had already switched off his mobile.

I was still crying when Adam phone at 10.05. It was wonderful to hear his voice.

'How did it go? Did you have to tell him?'

'No,' I said wiping my eyes with another tissue. 'He was going out to dinner with the boys, so he was in a hurry. I called him Dear and he queried that. I told him I wasn't feeling very well, thought I had drunk too much wine last night. Oh Darling, I felt such a bitch.'

'You are not a bitch, Sweetheart. Don't ever think that. That was the best thing to do.'

We talked a bit more. By this time my head was thumping, so Adam said he would call me at lunch time tomorrow.

'Take two aspirins my darling and go to bed.'

'Oh Adam, I love you so much,' I answered.

We both declared our love for each other again and we said goodnight.

I won't dwell on how the reunion went the next morning. Suffice to say Hal was devastated. I felt like a real bitch but I told him as gently as I could. After a lot of soul searching, he finally understood how I felt about him not being strong enough for me. He wished me all the luck in the world and told me I knew where to reach him if I ever needed him.

Adam and I had a lovely second wedding at an old house owned by one of our friends with all our family and friends to share our loving vows with us.

I finished my wine and looked across at my new husband. I know this time we will always communicate, and we have promised we will never go to bed angry at each other. We know for sure we will always be together, even if we still do argue at times.

LADY MADONNA MEETS THE MARTIANS
Bernie Dowling

For Lachlan Hurse

Petrie, north of Brisbane, winter, 1995
FOUR-year-old Ryan was teasing his sister, 6, patting her back quickly and repeatedly, as he had seen a mother do forcefully in the supermarket when her child was choking on a lolly.

Chloe accepted her brother's game for a while before calling for intervention from Mummy. Felicity Sailor brushed aside locks of her long blonde hair from her pretty oval face, revealing creases in her forehead, marking her 29 years of life in Queensland. 'Ryan, stop teasing your sister.' Felicity, better known as Flick, looked across at her son before continuing to rearrange a pile of bills, jotting down figures on a notepad and shaking her head at the impossible financial obligations.

'I wasn't giving her tea,' an offended Ryan said.

I could see that Flick was on the verge of losing it and offered half-hearted mediation. 'Maybe Ryan does not know what teasing means.'

'You're no help, Steele. Ryan knows what to tease means. I am always telling him not to tease his sister and I have explained what it means.'

This was Chloe's cue. 'Mum, Ryan's teasing me.' The girl sobbed softly and slowly upped the ante to full-blown tears.

'See what you've done.' Flick was accusing – me, not Ryan.

I was about to defend myself when 9-year-old Justin called from his room, 'Mum, where's my Marilyn Manson T-shirt. I have sports tomorrow and I need it.'

Despite Justin's continual insistence to the contrary, it was not really his room; he shared it with his brother. Mother and daughter had the other bedroom of the small rented house – small by Australian standards, perhaps not so much by European.

Justin and I were mates. When he told me his physical education teacher refused to allow him to wear his Manson T-shirt in sports, I pretended to be appalled. The predominately white-on-black logo had splotches of red. Justin was in the Red team for sports.

I suggested he tell his teachers he would take them to the international court of justice in The Hague if he was not allowed to wear his somewhat red T-shirt. I did not think he would do it. To be fair to me, he did not – precisely.

The note Flick showed me from PE teacher Mr Pendleby said Justin had threatened him with the tennis court of justice in The Hog. Felicity was hopping mad at me. I always seem to be in trouble with women. It takes a great deal of reflection to understand why. Usually I do not bother with such tedious self-criticism.

On that winter evening, I did ponder whether my visit to Flick's to see the Martians was wise. Flick's car registration had run out earlier in the week. I suggested Flick and Ryan could ride with me in the front of my one-seater Holden EH ute. The older kids could travel in the tray.

Flick said I was the most irresponsible man in the world. That hardly seemed likely but the prospect made me laugh. Felicity pulled the punch just as I retracted my head from the blow's obvious destination.

'We'll go in my car,' she said.

'I'll pay your registration tomorrow,' I offered.

'I know you haven't got any money, Steele. Whenever you win at the horses, you have that silly smirk on your face. It's not there.'

Wow, I should teach Flick how to play poker. She has a powerful read and her financial troubles could soon be over. But Flick does not like gambling. Her dead-beat ex-husband, Howdy, was a jockey as well as being thousands behind in his maintenance payments. The jockey still rode his share of winners though nowhere near as many as when he was Brisbane's top hoop a decade earlier. That was when Flick and I bonded over a race fix demanded by her father who had kidnapped his own daughter. It's a long story and there is no time for that now. We had Martians to see.

'I brought a cassette tape. Does the cassette player still work in the Falcon?' I asked. Flick owned a 1978 Ford Falcon, fourteen years younger than my Holden EH, though not as reliable.

'Of course it works. If it didn't I'd buy a CD player. I've got plenty of tapes so I don't need yours.'

'Yes, but I have one with *Lady Madonna* on it, in your honour.'

'*Lady Madonna*? Is that a Madonna song, Steele?'

I thought she was taking the piss. '*Lady Madonna*,' I said. 'Children at your feet...'

She shook her pretty head to signal zero recognition.

'The Beatles,' I said.

'Oh Steele, what are you listening to that old shit for? You're younger than me. It's embarrassing.'

Ever since Flick caught me watching a 1940s Hollywood film-noir on video, she has treated me like a cultural deviant. I cannot remember what movie it was, possibly *The Big Sleep* or *The Maltese Falcon*. I have seen each a dozen times. I should add it was in the privacy of my own flat where Flick sprung me. And I had made no effort to turn off the video player before I let her in.

On our Martian evening of that year of 1995, I had sat through a double feature of videos in Flick's house. The first was *Pocahontas* and the second was *Waterworld*. Flick said the Disney 'toon *Pocahontas* was for the kids. Who knew whom the Kevin Costner aqua opera was for – possibly Martians. Felicity's fave song of '95 was Seal's *Kiss from a Rose*, even though the R&B singer forgot to button his shirt for the promotional video. Obviously R&B did not stand for "robe and button". And I am copping roberta-flack for film noir and the Beatles.

Lady Madonna packed up the unregistered Falcon with the kids, dressed against the winter chill, and me. The engine spluttered into life. Flick received a single-parent's benefit from the government but had to work two part-time jobs to make ends meet. Her father, retired Russian racehorse trainer Bill Smith – don't ask about the English name – could help little financially but he did baby-sit when Felicity went to work. She did not tell her father about the Martians. He had kidnapped her in the past and he might concoct some crazy plan to make money from the aliens' visit.

I should say at this point I don't believe in aliens. Flick does not believe in aliens. Yet we were going to look for them and I guess you can blame me for that.

Flick told me she was probably tired from five hours of paid baby-sitting the night she saw the spaceship land in the bush off Narangba Rd. She pulled over at the side of the road to watch the pulsating silver light around the ship. She did not actually see the Martians.

'How did you know they were Martians?' I asked.

'I never said they were Martians. You did, Steele.'

'They could have been Venusians,' I said.

'I never said they were Martians. You did. And what the hell are Venusians?'

'From Venus. I think that's what they are called. But they were most probably Martians. They are more common, I believe.'

I am not sure why I said that. Neither of us believes in Martians.

We drove to where Felicity thought she had pulled over. In the headlights we saw recent car tracks on the clay beside the road. They could have come from the Falcon.

Flick pointed towards an area about 100 metres into the bush. There was a small circular clearing among the gum trees. A spaceship might land there but it would have to be tiny. Martians are small, aren't they?

I asked Flick how old the car battery was if we wanted to shine the high beam on the spot in the bush.

'The battery is two-years-old, but we have come all this way, so we have to take a chance.'

She swung the car to fully face the spot, put the lights on high beam and turned off the motor.

'Maybe you should have kept the motor running, I said. 'Might be less strain on the battery.'

'You think?'

'Dunno. I know nothing about cars. Leave it for the moment.'

Justin was the first to complain from the back seat. 'What are we doing here?'

Ryan wanted to go home to watch television and Chloe said the dark was scary.

'Steele's lost something,' Felicity told the children.

I said to Flick I heard her say "his marbles" under her breath.

She denied it and laughed. 'But I was sure thinking it. The Martians must have given you the power to read minds.'

I opened the passenger-side door.

'You're not going in there alone, Steele? Are you mad?'

I put on my best attempt at the earnest voice of the star of a low-budget sci-fi film. 'We must end this thing.'

Ryan pleaded from his corner of the back seat. 'I want to go too.'

That was not happening as Felicity had activated the child-proof locks on both back doors. As Ryan whimpered, Flick told me to hurry.

The grass was higher than it had looked from the car. I was glad I had worn boots but I trod carefully. The clearing too was larger than it seemed from the road.

The grass was flattened, though not in a circle. It was more like the vegetation had been trampled along a series of parallel paths. I leaned over to see if I could discern a crater. I though there should be a crater and some burnt areas around it, as in 1950s sci-fi movies. I heard Flick yelling at me to hurry up. I turned and my boot kicked a note on the ground. It was rectangular, about six inches long and a couple of inches wide. It looked like it bore someone's portrait inside an oval. I pocketed it.

Back at the car, I inspected the note in the headlights. It took a while to figure it out as I had never seen the like of it in my life. Flick asked what it was.

I hopped back in the car and said, 'The Martians left their calling card.' I placed the note in front of Flick's face. 'Lady Madonna, meet Benjamin Franklin.'

'Is that monopoly money?'

'I think not. If you take this US hundred-dollar bill to the bank, tomorrow, I believe the kind banker will give you enough Aussie moolah to pay your registration.'

'You don't think the Martians kidnapped someone and the victim dropped their money.'

'Possibly,' I said. 'But I would put my money on your good fortune coming courtesy of an American tourist venturing from the beaten track.'

We went back to Petrie and Flick put the kids to bed. Over coffee, we amused each other with fantastic tales of how the money landed in the bush at Narangba.

Neither of us had another Martian adventure. Ever.

A GRAVE ENDING
R. William Penshorn

RUGGEDLY handsome young Zack Butler sat with his pretty wife Ava at the breakfast table in their rented flat. Their cute one-year-old daughter, Belle was with them. She was in a high chair.

Zack stood up to take some bread to the toaster. 'This is pretty fancy-looking bread Honey,' he said.

'It was on special,' Ava replied.

'Thank God for that. This stuff usually costs an arm and a leg.'

'It's much better bread, all the same. It's a damn pity we can't have it all the time.'

'You know we're flat out making ends meet, Ava. Give me a break.'

'Why can't you get a better paying job? We could sure do with some more money.'

'The way everything is forever going up including the cost of our rent, even with overtime every day, we'd be flat out saving a damn cent. You know that.'

'Something's gotta give, that's all I can say,' Ava said. 'What sort of a future has poor little Belle got if we can't even afford to give her some decent bloody bread?'

Later that day, Zack was operating a jack hammer to break into the side of a concrete man-hole to allow for a new sewerage pipe connection. He thought to himself, 'How did I ever get to have a job like this? What a loser I've turned out to be.'

His thoughts went on to the morning's TV program which featured the incomes of top-billing movie stars and entertainers. To add to his fury it was announced that politicians were just awarded another rise, which, in many cases, exceeded his gross income. 'Something's wrong somewhere,' he grumbled.

At smoko he grabbed his Thermos flask and lunch box to sit with a few work mates under a partly shady tree by the roadside.

A low loader went by with a new Komatsu Excavator on board and this caused an older fellow in the gang named Charlie Hart to say, 'I should have bought m'self one of them years ago.

Those owner- operators make more in half a day than what we do in a week.'

'Why didn't you?' Zack asked.

'I spent all my money on cigarettes, booze and women,' Charlie answered. 'Wasted the rest.' Charlie smiled to show his brown teeth, stained with nicotine.

'I wouldn't mind getting myself one of those excavators,' Zack said.

'You'd have more chance of flying to Jupiter on your money, mate,' said Charlie. 'You'd have to win Lotto or rob a bank.'

'I can't even afford a ticket in Lotto,' Zack replied. 'Bubby's gotta have her milk.'

A week later, Zack's workmates were astonished to learn he had quit his job. 'I had some amazing luck at the casino and I'm taking my family on a well-deserved holiday,' he said.

He told Ava the construction company had paid everyone a bonus and he decided to try his luck at the casino. 'A little bird told me to play roulette,' he said. 'And I did.'

'A little bird?' quizzed Ava.

'It was no dumb parrot,' Zack grinned. 'I played my birthday number, 16. You wouldn't believe how many times it came up. I made a small fortune.'

After living it up for a week at the coast, Zack decided he must do something to secure his family's future.

During that time, newspapers and TV reports covered a mysterious bank robbery. Huge amounts of cash had gone missing without a trace. Police were mystified. Zack knew exactly how it had gone down. He was the mastermind and the sole executor of the criminal deed.

He put on a brave front but underneath it all, he was scared out of his wits. He vowed to himself he would never commit any such act again. The casino story was a pack of lies.

Soon after the holiday, he went to an earthworks-plant sales yard and invested in a brand new Komatsu Excavator and set up in business.

Before long he was busy digging trenches for pipelines, doing earthworks for roadways and estates plus some private jobs such as swimming pool excavations. The money rolled in.

Serendipity

On one occasion, while excavating for a household swimming pool, the lady of the house, an attractive young woman named Tamm Peretz, invited Zack in for a cup of tea. She was quick to let him know her husband Robert was away on a business trip and would not be back for a week. Zack was quick to read between the lines, and, as soon as he had devoured one lamington, two ginger nuts and a hot cup of tea, he found himself in her bed with both of them going for it.

When he arrived home that evening, Ava asked as she usually did, 'Did you have a good day, Honey?'

To which he replied, 'I guess so. I was hard at it all day, again.'

'You poor dear,' Ava said. 'Don't think I don't appreciate all the effort you put in for me.'

'It's because I love you, Darling,' said Zack.

'I know you do and you can show me just how much you do tonight,' Ava said with a sexy wink.

'Sure,' Zack answered.

Zack visited Tammy every day that week until Robert returned when she advised him he had better make himself scarce and forget any of it had ever happened.

'Thanks for the memories,' Zack said.

He bought a luxurious waterfront home at the Gold Coast where he, Ava and Belle spent many wonderful years. He and Ava wanted another child, hopefully a son, but fate had it that Ava never fell pregnant again.

Zack enjoyed the high life. He spent some time at the casino, dining out, seeing shows and gambling. He took a liking to playing roulette but he was now too cautious to become reckless. Sometimes he was lucky and if he felt the vibes that things were not going his way, he had the good sense to pull out.

Years passed. Zack kept himself fit by going on beach walks, working out at the gym and cycling. He could well have afforded to put on an operator for the Komatsu but he enjoyed using it and believed it kept him in touch with reality.

Ava kept her youthfulness. She liked to swim and play squash. One sport Zack and Ava enjoyed together was Ping Pong. Of course there were other activities they liked to jointly participate in.

Belle grew into her teens and became a gorgeous young woman. She was lovely and as fair as the rose of the summer, a true Belle. She went to ball-room dances, liked to ride her surf board and excelled in most things she took on. She had lots of male suitors but kept them all dangling on a string. She was popular with her women friends also and sometimes, to Zack's delight, she would invite them to stay with her at her parent's home for week-ends.

Zack would eye them amorously from a distance. It was too close to home to play Casanova.

Zack was not the saint Ava believed him to be. Sometimes, while paying a solo visit to the casino, he would approach women he considered desirable. If they agreed to his propositions, he would disappear somewhere into the night with a chosen one and have his way. Afterwards he would present them with a generous sum of cash and his parting words always were, 'Keep your mouth shut.'

One time at the roulette table Zack had an inkling number 16 was about to come up. He placed $100 on it and it did come up. 'You little beauty,' he exclaimed. 'That's what I like.'

A woman came to stand beside him. 'Half your luck,' she said. Zack turned to face her and was delighted to recognize Tammy Peretz. 'Tammy,' he said, 'It is you, isn't it? It's been a long time. How are you?'

'I'm not pregnant.'

'Ha ha, I can see that,' Zack chuckled. 'You're looking great.'

'But I was, pregnant that is,' Tammy went on.

'So you're a mother now, I take it. Is everything okay?'

'Everything's fine Zack. Robert and I are the proud parents of a fine young son.'

'Good for you. What did you call him?'

'We called him Jack. He looks a lot like you.'

'A handsome little devil eh? Ha ha.'

'That he is for sure,' Tammy agreed.

'How old is he?'

'Let's put it this way Zack. He was born about nine months after we had the pool installed. Are you catching on?'

'Holy Hell! You don't mean?'

'I'd put all the money you just won plus a whole lot more on it.'

'Holy Hell!'

'Don't worry your pretty little head about it, Zack. Robert hasn't got a clue Jack is not his and I, sure as the Pope is a Roman Catholic, have no intention of telling him.'

'I, I don't know what to say,' Zack muttered. 'I...I always wanted a son.'

'So did I Zack. You can't win 'em all.'

'I, I'd like to meet him.'

'I'll bet you would, maybe someday. I've got to go now; Robert's waiting. See you around.'

More years passed by. Zack never saw Tammy again nor met Jack. He never let on to Ava, Belle or anyone about their existence.

The time arrived when Zack decided he had more money than he would ever need so he decided to retire. He daydreamed about what a glorious retirement laid in store and placed an ad in a newspaper, *Excavator for sale.*

A handsome young man named Rafe Penzhurst answered the ad. Rafe's father William Penzhurst, had been the manager of the bank Zack robbed many years earlier.

Unlike his father, Rafe had always wanted to be involved in an outdoor career. His family were wealthy enough to set him up. Zack arranged to meet Rafe at a vacant paddock to demonstrate how the machine worked.

'You won't regret buying this,' Zack said. 'It has sure provided handsomely for my family and me for more years than I wish to think about.'

'You sure have kept it in good nick,' said Rafe.

'Treat it with plenty of TLC and it will stay that way.'

Zack dug a hole about the size of an average grave and suggested Rafe try his hand at the controls. Zack stood beside the hole to give directions when Rafe boarded the Komatsu. He pulled a lever. 'What does this one do? 'Rafe asked.

The excavator arm swung swiftly. The bucket hit Zack with a firm thud. He fell into the hole, stone dead.

WILD LILIES

Bakthi Ross

BURDEN on a child and neglect by her mother reflect through the child's emotions. A child's behaviour changes without input from the mother. The child's thinking changes course.

Sarah was innocently playing with the animals and established an emotional connection with them. Slowly an emotional exchange between animals and the child had a hold on Sarah. A smile was the only enjoyment for a neglected lonely girl. Enthusiasm towards animals and the cuddles she gave to those animals were the happy moments she enjoyed.

Motherly love expected by a child was rejected and Sarah learned to love the animals and received affection from them. Cuddling and enjoying the warmth of a mother is important to a child but Sarah had connections of love and care only from the animals. Sarah's thinking and her knowledge were gained without the help of her parent or other human beings.

Sarah waltzed back and forth to the farmyard while her mother could not care less about where she was or what she was doing. Sarah comfortably lived with the birds and the animals. At the farm she was curiously looking, touching and feeling the sense of closeness she was desperately seeking. The normality of a childhood was flowing in a different form. Sarah was mentally grasping things that are not normal for a child.

A performance and narration of a verse that was unheard by anyone should have made the child's mother pay attention to the child. Sarah trotted up and down and sang a song of the wild lilies. She made it up so correctly, better than any famous poet or professor. She sang it again and again until her mother raised her head up and stared at that neglected child.

> *Wild lilies white as snow,*
> *Narrow valley,*
> *Blooming flowers,*
> *Butterflies and bees*
> *Tarnished the white bed of flowers.*

A gentle grin on her mother's face showed satisfaction. She was proud of that child. You do not have to tame a child to learn things. Sarah learned things without the help of her parent.

She was part of nature and part of the animal world. The mother did not understand the desperation of that child, lacking motherly love and looking for it elsewhere. Sarah could be a poet or she could be a writer. It was not all because of her learning things as a child. It was also because of lack of love, that unspoken pain in a child's life that no one in the future could ever compensate. A neglected child.

Sarah's mother was kneading the flour, singing and enjoying her passion for cooking. She liked to feed the family. She did not have any spare time to enjoy the family with household chores taking priority. She smiled in the kitchen and sang while she cooked and felt satisfied if everyone enjoyed the meals she cooked. That was the only satisfaction she expected from them. Sometimes she told them, 'if I feed you you'll grow on your own.'

It was like she was giving plants their basic needs but she could not give them the light of life. A mother's needs, a neglected child could understand. But as a mother she failed to understand the child. She went about her daily routine and would not connect with the child.

Sarah's mother was a sad person but she satisfied herself in some things that did not really cater for her own needs. Sometimes her daughter would see her outbursts of tears, rolling like bundles of stored emotions. She cried for hours and then she was calm again as if she had got rid of her worries. The next day she again cooked to get some satisfaction.

Sarah tried to get closer to her mother but her mother did not understand her. Since Sarah got more attention from the animals than her mother she stopped seeking parental affection. It did leave a blank space in her life but she never knew that it could have some emotional effect on her.

She became an artist and her paintings reflected her emotional status as a child. She discovered the importance of the emotional link between a child and a parent and how it leaves recurring images in your emotional pictures.

She thought about Picasso and why some of his paintings created a sense of ugliness. Why did he paint those distorted images? As Sarah was, he, as a child, might have been going through some emotional pain that he did not recognise but which resurfaced in his paintings in the later years. The unidentifiable pain that you could only paint on a blank canvas.

As time went on Sarah's mother expected more of her. She wanted her to be successful. If she was not successful, if she could not hold a job, her mother would not blame herself but blame Sarah. The affection expected was one sided.

'Can humans live alone without connections to others? Can we paint the painful emotions and feel free? Why do we need affection from others? *Why that link needs to exist in some form is because it is the first form of communication before spoken words,* thought Sarah.

Sarah filled her emotional blank space with paintings, poems and writings. Her art works and poems had an emotional connection to her childhood.

> *A picture without a thousand words,*
> *A poem without salvation,*
> *A child's journey without guidance,*
> *A sea without calmness,*
> *A maestro without music,*
> *In the playing field of life.*

Sarah backed away from human affection and found solace in her work. As for her mother, she continued shielding her feelings and needs. When all the children had gone away from home, her mother did not have anyone to cook for so she was lost. She did not sing and hated cooking. Eating alone was even harder for her. Looking at her empty dining table, she revisited the past. She smiled alone and cried alone, thinking about the past.

Past memories, past life, her life standing still, not moving. After a lifetime of family and home, she had to face the world as a lonely woman. She talked to the birds and she talked to the cat as she sought that emotional connection with the animals. She woke up to feed the cat and the day started with her talking to it. Was it enough of an emotional connection or would she go mad without a family? Sarah's mother wanted that emotional connection with her daughter and other human beings but she failed to seek it. Living alone meant she talked to things and animals. She sought that emotional connection but somehow it was not enough. Sarah could feel the desperation in her mother.

Sarah could not fill her mother's empty space but she filled her own needs with art, poetry and prose.

Sarah could see her deprivation through her paintings and in her writings. She learnt to realise what was lacking in her life. How her mother could make herself happy and live a fulfilled life, she did not know. Sarah could see her mother's loneliness. Life was there because it had to be, not because her mother wanted it.

Are we incapable of living alone?

If Sarah's mother wrote a poem how would it sound? Would this be her poem – the one Sarah wrote for her?

A ballroom without dancing feet,
Twilight memories,
A blushing face,
She moved her lace and waved
At her past.
A silent moment brings her back,
Now the tears control her
And she sits and sobs the moment.

Our memories, our feelings, our pain, our lives are the raw materials of our writing, our paintings, our songs. Sarah understood herself as a person with her own needs but her mother could not understand hers. Whenever she visited Sarah all she talked about was the past. When humans become lonely do they talk about their past more than the future? Sarah knew that her mother could not face the future alone. She had lost interest in life. Her mother lived her life within the shadows of the past.

She did enjoy Sarah's paintings, prose and poems but she did not recognise the pain and relief in her daughter's works. Serendipity! A white cloud, a white lily, a child is on her way to being a poet.

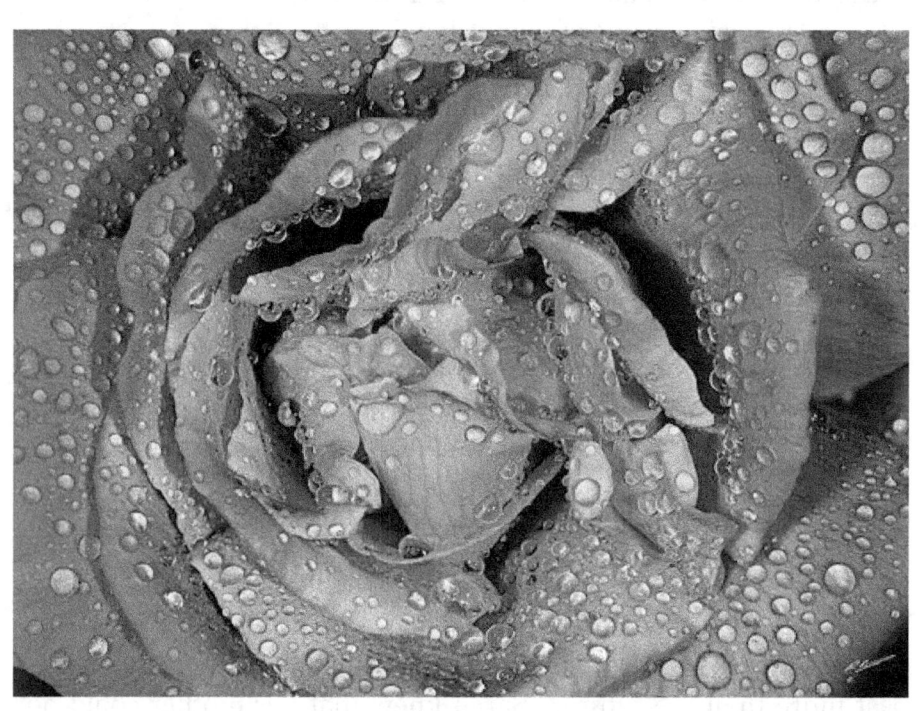

CELEBRATION

Pamela Harris

THERE are numerous forms of celebrations, such as weddings, births, birthdays, graduations and promotions but the following is one of the most beautiful. It is the CELEBRATION OF SOUND.

For me, 1957 was a wonderful year filled with happiness and hope. In that year I married Claude. Not only did I marry the love of my life but later that same year my cousin Norma married Claude's brother Ray.

My husband was a carpenter and he built our home and that of his brother and sister-in-law. We lived in a single unlined garage while Claude built our house. That way he could work on our home after work and in the evenings. We were young and, although it was winter, we did not mind the few discomforts.

The year 1958 was also filled with happiness. Ray and Norma celebrated their first child, a boy Stephen. A few months later Claude and I were ecstatic at the arrival of our first child, also a son Garry. The future knew no bounds. The two brothers, who were always very close, were as happy as any siblings could be.

A year of sorrow followed in 1959 as I lost my beloved Claude after a very short illness. With no social support as there is today, I had to just get on with life but that is another story.

In 1960 Norma and Ray welcomed a daughter, Donna. She was a beautiful child, placid, happy and no trouble at all, but the parents discovered that she had been born deaf. My mother-in-law relayed the news to me and said the family was devastated but were also very hopeful that something may be able to be done for their beloved daughter.

Another daughter, Glenda, arrived for Norma and Ray in 1962. Hopes were high that this little girl would not suffer the same fate as her sister.

One afternoon when Glenda was just at the sitting-alone stage and Norma had to go out for a short time and left the children at home with Ray Arriving home, she alighted from the car and she heard the alarm clock. She thought, *what on earth is Ray doing with an alarm at this time in the afternoon?* Opening the door she saw Ray sitting on the floor with Glenda. Her husband was holding the alarm clock behind Glenda's head before looking up at his wife with tears in his eyes. 'She cannot even hear the damn alarm,' he said.

When Donna was about four-years-old she was placed in boarding school for the deaf in Newcastle as there were no facilities in the rural city in which we lived. Nuns taught Donna to lip read.

Norma and Ray later had another child. I will never forget the look of hope on Ray's face when he called in to let me know that the new addition to the family had arrived. He said, 'It is a boy.' This little boy was, to the delight of all, like his older brother. This little boy was not at all hearing impaired.

Not long after the arrival of their fourth child, Ray fell ill. After an operation, the family decided to move to Newcastle where it would be possible for them to have their daughters at home. The girls could attend the convent as day students for their schooling and continue to be taught to lip read.

Sadly, Ray passed away, and left Norma with the four children. She never remarried and used to laugh that who would take on a woman with four children including two with such problems.

The girls grew. Although they could lip read, it is almost impossible for any of us to understand the trauma of rearing two deaf children. If you looked out the window and noticed some childish adventure being undertaken by energetic children could be dangerous, you could not simply call out to alert them of the danger. You had to stop what you were doing and go to them. Norma was an amazing Mother and the four children to this day all remain extremely close to her.

Both girls on leaving school were able to obtain employment sewing in a clothing factory and were able to become to a certain extent self-sufficient.

Unfortunately Norma and I lost contact with her moving to Newcastle, and me remarrying and eventually moving to Queensland. Except for a very occasional card or phone call, we had no contact with each other. We were both very busy bringing up our children and involved with our busy working lives.

The year 2012 arrived and I guess now being in our seventies I had become sentimental and decided to make a telephone call to Norma. I had heard that her girls had married but in both instances these had not been successful. I also wanted to obtain her permission to relate an incident in the life of one of the girls.

Well what a telephone call that was. It was then that Norma related to me what I consider one of the most wonderful stories I have ever heard.

Glenda had married and had a son. When the marriage fell apart, Glenda moved home so that her Mum could assist in the upbringing of her beloved baby boy.

Norma said that she had such a wonderful relationship with this grandson as there were times when she was able to discuss matters with him and assist with his homework. She was able to communicate him in ways which were not always possible with his own Mother. She drove him to football practice and matches as Glenda's deafness meant she was unable to hold a driver's license.

Glenda, now in her late forties, read of the progress in the medical field of Cochlear implants. She wondered if she was too old for such a procedure.

She had made extensive enquiries and had an assessment. It was possible for her to have a Cochlear implant. The wait was lengthy but what was that after she had already waited almost fifty years.

Norma finally received the telephone call from the Professor advising that it was now Glenda's turn. She had to accept straight away or once again go to the bottom of the list.

The decision was easy.

Norma was advised that the procedure could not be performed in Newcastle. She would have to travel to Sydney. This was not going to be an obstacle; the family would be in Sydney at the designated time and place.

There was much excitement and anticipation not only by Glenda and Norma but from the whole family.

The procedure was performed. Doctors advised Norma and Glenda that all looked good but it would take three weeks before the implant could be turned on, so they would know for certain. The turning-on would be done in Newcastle; they would not need to return to Sydney for it.

Those three weeks seemed like a lifetime. Eventually, the BIG DAY arrived. Glenda was accompanied by her mother, two brothers, a nephew and most especially her son. One can only imagine the anticipation and nerves in that room as they waited for the procedure. The medical staff said that this was the largest entourage any patient had ever had at such a procedure.

They turned on the implant.

Norma said that it was the most astonishing sight – the look on the face of her Daughter who had not even heard the minutest sound in all the years of her life. She had never heard her own child cry, laugh or talk. For the first time Glenda heard SOUND. It was her Son who actually recorded this momentous occasion.

There was a lot of learning for Glenda. She had never heard voices, and did not know the sounds of words she had lip-read. She began to modify the way she herself pronounced some words.

Glenda learned the sounds of a moving car, a washing machine, a kettle boiling: all the things the hearing enabled take for granted. Glenda could now watch a movie and follow the storyline. Norma said her daughter would walk through the house and say, 'Isn't that wonderful' to the most ordinary of sounds which we take for granted and sometimes even complain about.

This is what I truly believe is a celebration – a CELEBRATION OF SOUND – which must have been as exciting for Norma as it was for her daughter.

Glenda's older sister Donna has decided that she too will investigate the possibility of having a Cochlear implant. Her assessment should happen any time soon.

Cochlear implants are wonderful words to hear for those that have lived in a world of silence for so long.

Hearing, a final note: Although not the inventor of the Cochlear implant, Australian Professor Graeme Clark and his University of Melbourne colleagues developed the Australian prototype bionic ear, first implanted into Rod Saunders, in 1978.

THE AUTHORS

Long John Best was born in England and came to Australia, aged 10. After discharge from the Air Force, he worked many jobs, including the most rewarding of working with people with a disability. Recognised as one of Australia's premier bush poets, he has performed in America. Against the grain of perversity in Australian nicknames, Long John is tall.

Bernie Dowling is a Pine Rivers journalist and author. His books include fiction and non-fiction. His latest works are the musical play *Dagworth Day*, (with Gloria Swenson), another musical *Christian and Humble*, and his first novel, *Iraqi Icicle*. His neo-noir detective Steele Hill returns for this anthology but is engaged in less deadly pursuits, for a change.

Rebekah Dowling, began the story in this anthology at eighteen while studying Creative Writing in New York and missing her home country terribly. Growing up outside of Brisbane in a country town, she has always felt strong connection with the Australian landscape and people. This was accentuated through her Grandmother's stories of growing up in rural Barcaldine and her own childhood memories of camping under gumtrees, eating damper, boiling the billy and hearing Dad recite Banjo Patterson poems.

Maurice Hardy is a musician and song writer in the country genre. Recovering from a serious illness, he wrote a 95,000 word novel *Shadows of Perfection*. He is seeking a publisher. Maurice's story for this anthology continues his fascination with the interplay of nature and families.

Pamela Harris was born in a small town of Nundle in N.S.W. She spent most of her childhood investigating hills outside the town.

As an adult she worked for forty years in the aviation industry. She retired at 67-years-old but she was approached to do contract work for an aviation facility in Cairns. She finally managed to retire permanently just before turning 70.

Ronald Holt retired from the Queensland public sector in 2006 after more than forty years' service – the last 14 years in the Office of Fair Trading. He wrote numerous reports and departmental correspondence on a wide range of issues and is now applying those skills to his love of creative writing. He has edited four anthologies, 2007, 2009, 2011 and 2013 for the Arana Writers' Group. He has had short stories published on Anzac Cove and global warming.

Sharyn Hutchinson is a writer of mystery and children's stories. The proud mother of five children, she wrote many of her books to inspire the two eldest boys to read. Now the family's house renovations are complete, she is concentrating on her writing again.

Belinda Janz has written short stories, poetry and stories for children as well as assisting in writing a radio play. She has won short-story competitions and has been published in Australia and overseas in magazines and anthologies. Her other interests include sewing, craft work, ancient history studies, cooking, reading, spirituality, massage and helping people.

David MacLaughlin began writing for a staff magazine when he came fourth from world-wide entries for a travel article. Writing took a back seat as David became active in choral and Celtic choirs and musical theatre. After that it was time to give writing its proper priority in things cultural. As a member of Arana Writers' Group, David has contributed to the group's three anthologies with articles factual, humorous, some fiction and travel tales.

Vera Murray was born in Allora, Queensland. She has been writing since her school days. She is a former Pine Rivers Shire Councillor. She has edited a magazine overseas. While running the Writer's Circle group in Pine Rivers, she edited and published three anthologies. Her book *Move Over James Bond and Other Stories* and her first novel *Leap Year: Blood Lust* were recently published.

Lorraine Noscov has had short stories published in the anthologies *Write Out of King's Cottage* by The Writer's Circle of Pine Rivers. In 2009 she published her book *Memoirs of a Vigilante*. As a child, she was an avid writer. As an adult, she prefers to write stories based on fact and real life experiences.

Anne Olsson is a remedial therapist living and working in Pine Rivers. She has been an enthusiastic actor on the amateur stage and, in recent years, an eager world traveller. Her poetry and articles have been published in newspapers and magazines.

R. William Penshorn has travelled the world but still calls Australia home. Now retired, he spent most of his working years involved in surveying and civil engineering projects. He has written several movie scripts and is waiting for Spielberg or Luhrmann to come knocking. His interests include comic collecting, classic automobiles, rock 'n' roll, art, surfing, and, of course, writing.

Raelene Purtill has, in her imagination, a husband of nineteen years, three teenage children and a suburban existence, north-west of Brisbane. In the real world, she writes. Short stories are her preferred medium although she has produced plays and poems. She is a member of two writing groups, Strathpine Writers Group and Vanguard Writers, a group formed following a course at the Queensland Writers' Centre. Her blog is raelenep.blogspot.com.au

Bakthi Ross is a member of the Caboolture Writer's Link. She started writing because of a dream and has written many children's books. Her ebooks are available at www.appspublisher.com. A mother of two children, she lives at Morayfield in Moreton Bay Region.

Brenda Simcox-Hunt came from England as a teenager with her parents in 1952. She is widowed with five children and eight grandchildren. She has been writing for about 10 years and has had stories and poems published by local publishers. She is working on a book of short stories, two novels and three children's books

Margaret Taylor was born many moons ago in England. She has lived in the North of England, the South of England, America and New Zealand. She currently lives in Brisbane, Australia, with her family. She writes when she remembers to, and reads a lot of books because she is in a book club. Margaret is retired from the workforce but not from life or a challenge.

Phone 617 3264 2311
Email peter@petercampbellrealty.com
Web www.petercampbellrealty.com

THE ILLUSTRATORS

RUSSELL BROWN is an Australian newspaper and artistic photographer. He has had exhibitions in Australia and overseas. Last year, Russell's work was included in the *Salon de la Photo* exhibition in Paris. One of his works at Paris, *Silent Sorrow,* is reproduced in this anthology along with a number of his more acclaimed photographs, selected to illustrate stories. He is the author of two books and supplied the cover image for the Bernie Dowling novel *Iraqi Icicle.* Visit http://www.russbrownart.com

KEN ARMSTRONG studied at the Dundee College of Art in Scotland before pursuing a diverse career path in illustration, journalism, script writing, magazine editing, and photography, not to mention a number of years in the UK military. Ken is at home with drawing, painting (mostly in oils) and has embraced digital art. His landscapes and portraits are in several private collections and his pastel portraits have proved very popular. He was the inaugural president of the Arts Alliance of Pine Rivers.

MARION MACLAUGHLIN has had photography as one of her hobbies since she received her first Box Brownie camera when she was 8-years-old. Over the years her hobby mainly translated into holiday snaps but since her retirement six years ago she has become more serious and adventurous about it. She uses an SLR camera and experiments with night photography, portraits, macro shots and photo editing, as well as taking important photos of the grandchildren. She is an award winner at local Samford and Pine Rivers Shows.

LEONIE ROMBOUT was born in Amsterdam, The Netherlands, and her family immigrated into Australia in the mid-1960s. Over the past forty-odd years, Leonie has been creating works of art in different media – painting, charcoals, pastels, mixed media, silver jewellery, pottery and photography. For much of that time, Leonie has held down a "real" job in administration which "at least pays the bills".

www.ingramcontent.com/pod-product-compliance
Lightning Source LLC
Chambersburg PA
CBHW070559180626
46817CB00005B/1905